The Human Givens Approach Series is a range of best-selling books, each of which explores a recognised psychological or be-havioural problem and shows in clear, non-jargonistic language how to treat it effectively with psychological interventions.

Release from Anger is the fourth title in the series, which includes: *How to Lift Depression ... Fast; Freedom from Addiction: The secret behind successful addiction busting* and *How to Master Anxiety: all you need to know to overcome stress, panic attacks, phobias, trauma, obsessions and more*. The next planned title will cover autism and Asperger's syndrome. (The series is part of a larger nationwide effort to move counselling, psy-chotherapy and education away from ideology and more into line with scientific findings about how the brain works and what people really need to live fulfilling lives.)

Joe Griffin is a research psychologist with graduate and post-graduate degrees from the LSE. He is hugely influential in the world of psychotherapy and is director of studies at the Human Givens Institute. He is co-author with Ivan Tyrrell of numerous titles including *How to Lift Depression ... Fast; Freedom from Addiction; How to Master Anxiety; Dreaming Reality: How dreaming keeps us sane or can drive us mad;* and *Human Givens: A new approach to emotional health and clear thinking.*

Ivan Tyrrell is the Principal of MindFields College, the only specialist college in the UK dedicated to the practical application of psychological knowledge. Each year over 12,500 professionals, including psychotherapists, counsellors, social workers, psychologists, nurses, doctors, psychiatrists, occupational therapists, youth workers, teachers, NHS and social welfare staff, attend its courses.

Denise Winn is a journalist specialising in psychology and medicine, and editor of the *Human Givens* journal.

Release from
anger

Practical help for controlling
unreasonable rage

Change is much easier
than you think...

Joe Griffin & Ivan Tyrrell

with Denise Winn

Release from
anger

A practical handbook

PUBLISHING

Joe Griffin & Ivan Tyrrell

with Denise Winn

PUBLISHING

First published in Great Britain 2008

Published by HG Publishing, an imprint of Human Givens Publishing Ltd,
Chalvington, East Sussex, BN27 3TD, United Kingdom.
www.humangivens.com

A catalogue record for this book is available from the British Library.

ISBN-13: 978-1-899398-07-2

Typeset in Book Antiqua and Conduit Condensed.
Printed and bound in Great Britain by CPI Antony Rowe.
Index by Indexing Specialists (UK) Ltd.

*"Let us not look back in anger
or forward in fear,
but around in awareness."*

JAMES THURBER

CONTENTS

Acknowledgements

We would like to thank Paula Bruce,
Mark Evans, David Grist, Christine Paul, Julian
Penton, Pat Williams and Pamela Woodford for
contributing some of the case histories in this
book, and our editor, Jane Tyrrell, for her
many thoughtful contributions, clarity
of expression and eye for detail.

Time to take charge

*P*URE ANGER is terrifying to behold in others and wildly overwhelming when it erupts in ourselves. But it is an emotion that we are all genetically programmed to experience; it evolved aeons ago as a survival mechanism to enable creatures like us to stand their ground under threat. And it can still be useful today: to motivate us to do something about a situation, for example, or when we occasionally need it to defend ourselves. But when it flares up inappropriately and rages out of control for no good reason, it is highly dangerous – as you almost certainly know if you have picked up this book.

Stress overload, generated by the way we live now, accounts for much of the increase in the expressions of anger in society. In today's stressful modern world (where we are driven to earn money *and* accumulate debt, where our innate needs are frequently undermined and time for reflection is hard to find), few of us live in the type of close and caring community in which most potential causes for anger outbursts can be diffused naturally before they do damage. And, as we are forced to engage with more and more systems that automate and dehumanise our work and social life, and endless red tape and regulations govern how we do the simplest of things, it is not surprising that even those who think of themselves as mild-tempered are driven to distraction from time to time and blow their tops.

For many other people, however, the cause of anger is more deep-seated and violent outbursts may occur seemingly out of the blue, due to reminders, conscious or not, of traumatic past experiences.

It is always devastating and frightening to experience anger outbursts that you feel powerless to control. It is equally devastating and frightening to be on the receiving end of uncontrolled anger – with considerable damage often done, as a result, to your confidence, self-esteem and sense of personal safety. As you are probably well aware, uncontained anger causes major upsets in relationships and family life, crises at work, college or school, and problems in coping with life generally. It also badly affects your physical and mental health. And if anger turns to violence, it can, quite literally, be a matter of life and death (as the increasing reports of murderous attacks on people who have been kicked to death show).

Perhaps you say, "I can't help myself", if you repeatedly lose your cool, or think you should forgive others who become aggressive or violent because they can't help themselves, either: they don't mean it really, despite the pain they cause you – and, perhaps, the black eye and broken ribs. But anger does *not* come out of the blue, nor is it ever inexplicable or unmanageable.

This book will help you to understand the causes of over-the-top anger that put you and/or others at risk. It explains why sometimes our actions and reactions seem to wind

> **66** Anger does *not* come out of the blue, nor is it ever inexplicable or unmanageable. **99**

other people up and lead to furious, regretted, rows with those we love, work with etc. – and why what *they* do may push the buttons that trigger anger in ourselves. By reading it you could find out some things that surprise you. If this is the case, remember that life rarely works how we think it does.

If you ever feel at the mercy of anger – your own or other people's – you will discover that you have the power to disarm or deal with it. We will show you how to stop being taken over by anger, how to keep yourself safe from anger in others, how to defuse inappropriate anger, and how to prevent resentments and annoyances from escalating into bitter or dangerous confrontations.

We have successfully used the methods we describe with countless clients over the years. They are highly effective because they involve working *with* the givens of human nature, instead of trying to struggle against them, as often happens. (For instance, no amount of reasoning with a person who is in a blind rage will ever calm them down.) We call this way of working the human givens approach and it underpins all the ideas and information we use and teach.

Whether you are on the receiving end of aggression – from a partner or parent, boss or colleague, customer or neighbour – or whether you are struggling to understand and control anger in yourself, you will find this book full of fascinating facts and insights, as well as simply explained techniques to put into practice.

> " ... you will have the knowledge and skills to control anger, instead of letting *it* control you. "

Some people prefer to back up what they learn with professional help, so we have also included guidance on where to seek effective therapy and what to expect from it.

Excessive anger and aggression, delivered by you or else directed at you, can ruin your life and that of others. But if you absorb and use what you can learn from these pages, you will have the knowledge and skills to control *it*, instead of letting it control you. There's no better time than now to reclaim your life.

PLEASE NOTE: To protect confidentiality, the biographical details in the various case histories used in this book have been changed.

PART 1

Understanding anger

*A*NGER can erupt in many ways. Sometimes it creeps up on you without you even noticing, building up inside like steam in a pressure cooker. Maybe you have had a trying day, which started with sleeping through the alarm clock, then missing the bus to work or finding the car wouldn't start. Or maybe one of the children forgot something crucial that they needed for school and you had to turn back and get it, making you late for whatever you had to do next. Then perhaps someone – a colleague, a parent at the school gate, or a stranger whom you accidentally obstruct for a second on the street – passes an unkind remark (at least, that's the way you read it) and you feel unsettled and a little threatened afterwards. Other little things continue to go wrong throughout the day, causing you to feel more pressured, more uncertain that you can cope and more out of control until, suddenly, it finally gets too much and – BANG – you lose your temper over some tiny, tiny thing! Perhaps you let rip at an innocent shop assistant or a stunned colleague, your bemused partner or shocked child. And later you feel so bad and ashamed, because you know that your reaction was uncalled for, and you have hurt someone unforgivably.

Or else you might find you get angry a lot. "It's just how I am" you say, "how I've always been" – at least, that's what you think. It's because you don't tolerate fools gladly, you tell yourself, and anyway, there is so much to get angry about – poor service, shoddy goods, bad manners. But perhaps you have noticed yourself becoming even more intolerant as time goes on, or that other people don't get angry in similar circumstances? Maybe you have a constantly simmering sense of resentment about virtually everything, which is tarnishing your outlook on life and leaves you ever ready to explode. Perhaps someone important to you has told you that you need to get a grip on yourself ...

Or are your anger outbursts a complete shock to you? Something ridiculously minor will trigger one off and you end up having a stupid row with your family or friends, ruining what should have been a happy occasion. Or else a 'red mist' descends and you just explode – sometimes seemingly over nothing. At that moment you are consumed by your rage, yet have no idea *why* at all. In your mind there is no question that you are right and your response – the delivery of a barrage of verbal insults or even blows – is completely justified. But then, when you have calmed down, you are utterly shocked and mystified by what you did, and find yourself pleading yet again for forgiveness, especially if it is loved ones that you have hurt. Or perhaps you are so ashamed that you cannot own up to your feelings of guilt, and say nothing at all – and gradually the emotional distance between you and those you love grows.

> 66 At that moment you are consumed by your rage, yet have no idea *why* at all. 99

Or maybe you have a violent temper which, when it bursts out, sometimes even lands you in trouble with the police. You know you have got to find a way to curb it but you just don't know how. Or perhaps it is your child's explosive anger that you don't understand and don't know how to cope with.

Perhaps you live with someone with a violent temper and are often on the receiving end of physical abuse. It is terrifying, shocking, yet always so seemingly out of character. "He only does it when he is drunk." "He doesn't mean it; he is so apologetic afterwards." And so you go on putting up with it and, the more you put up with it, the more powerless you feel and the more you may blame *yourself* for causing such rage.

Whatever the cause of the anger or the form it takes – and whether the anger is yours or you get the brunt of it – you know it is ruining your life, as well as hurting others. And, try whatever you may, you have never been able to take back control ... *till now*.

Wouldn't it be great to know *why* you are at the mercy of excessive anger and to discover that you already have all the tools you need to take back control? There is always an explanation for an anger outburst, even if, at the moment, it is hidden from you. Once you understand it, you can learn how to change your responses – those that make *you* uncontrollably angry or trigger inappropriate anger in others – and, also, to realise whether or not you are to blame for it. Sometimes it is others who need help. Whatever the case, it is urgent that you take action because anger can be a killer.

> 66 There is always an explanation for an anger outburst, although it may be hidden from you at the moment. 99

The impact of excessive anger

At work: Stress, which can manifest itself in anger, anxiety or depression, is one of the leading causes of work-related illness, accounting for a third of all new episodes of ill health. One person in five has suffered bullying at work, according to the Chartered Institute of Personnel and Development. (Teachers are one particularly vulnerable group. Some 87,610 children were excluded from England's secondary schools in 2005/6 for physical or verbal assaults on teachers, the equivalent of 2.7 per cent of all pupils. But on top of that teachers can sometimes face assaults and abuse from out-of-control parents and even bullying from colleagues.) One of the main reasons people give for unhappiness in the workplace, and for leaving their jobs, is poor communication, which may result in frustrated anger outbursts from bosses or colleagues. But small frustrations all take their toll, too, often building into something bigger. A survey by the Britannia Building Society in late 2007 found that 9 out of 10 workers were infuriated by actions of their colleagues, such as 'stealing' cups, talking loudly on mobile phones or 'pulling sickies'.

On accidents: People who are in the grip of anger do not pay proper attention. As a result, they are more prone to accidents. A recent American study by the National Highway Traffic Safety Administration showed that road rage is implicated in two out of three fatal accidents and is the main cause of death on the roads. Angry people may also become careless in their use of dangerous implements or machinery.

On violence: Out-of-control anger considerably raises the risk of resorting to violence. Newspapers are always reporting horrifying statistics. For instance, 1 in 17 drivers has been physically threatened or attacked. Every three days, in the UK, a woman dies as a result of domestic violence. Public servants are at particular risk and very often it is caring professionals who are on the receiving end of others' violence.

Although attacks on fire fighters are now so commonplace that many go unreported, the Fire Brigades Union estimates that there are at least 40 attacks against fire fighters responding to emergencies every week, many of them serious and violent. And they are not alone: over 1,000 such attacks were also made against ambulance crews, although those figures are dwarfed by the number of attacks on mental health care and learning disability staff who reported over 41,000 serious violent incidents (NHS Counter Fraud and Security Management Service). A recent British Medical Association survey found that at least a third of doctors have been verbally or physically attacked, with some suffering serious injuries. Of 3,000 nurses surveyed by the

> **66** Anger raises cholesterol levels and can result in damaged or blocked arteries ... **99**

Royal College of Nursing, a quarter said they had been physically attacked and more than half believed that the risk of violent anger attacks is increasing dramatically. *

On relationships: People who get angry always think they are right (we will explain why later) and that leads them to denigrate other people's views and downgrade the importance of other people's rights and needs. As successful relationships depend on the mutual satisfaction of the needs of everyone involved, anger undermines relationships. As angry people are highly critical, their cruel barbs, over time, are also highly likely to damage their partners' or children's self-esteem.

On health: Excessive or chronic anger takes an enormous toll on the body.

- Anger increases the risk of hypertension, raises cholesterol levels and can result in damaged or blocked arteries (arteries harden faster in people who spend a lot of time feeling hostile or angry), causing or aggravating heart disease. It used to be thought that people described as having 'Type A' personalities (go-getting and driven) were much more likely to suffer from heart disease than so-called laid back and relaxed 'Type B' personality types. But it is now well known that it isn't the go-getting and drive that cause problems: the big risk factor is *chronic anger* and *hostility*,

---

* Most of these statistics have been drawn from reports in *The Sunday Times Magazine*, July 16, 2006 and *The Sunday Telegraph*, February 17, 2008.

which often, but by no means always, driven people tend to suffer from.

- Anger also affects our immune system, reducing its ability to defend the body against infection. One revealing experiment, conducted at the former Common Cold Unit in Wiltshire, showed that people are more susceptible to cold viruses if they have been involved in a major argument in the previous 48 hours. It is also known that people who suffer from chronic anger take longer to recover from major injury or surgery.

If anger is such a dangerous emotion, you may well be wondering by now, why does it exist? As we noted in our introduction, anger does have its uses. So, before we can understand where it all goes wrong, we need to take a moment to examine more closely what nature originally designed anger to do for us.

Anger is an ancient survival mechanism

Anger is a resource given to us by nature to enable us to defend ourselves, our kith and kin, and our territory. This was absolutely crucial long ago, before civilisation, when enemy tribes would try to muscle in on each other's patches. If we hadn't been genetically programmed to stand up and fight for ourselves and defend our homes and loved ones, we would soon have been trampled on and sent packing or physically destroyed. In modern times, one of the most vicious types of dispute that can develop is still a dispute between neighbours – usually about some infringement of territory, such as blocking a shared drive, branches from next-door's tree overhanging the garden, a fence post a millimetre across a shared boundary, music being played too loud, and so on. It is in the nature of all living creatures to try to expand their territory – their 'power base'. So, if we don't stand up for ourselves or make our boundaries clear, not only will other people walk all over us but even our pets will do so, too!

Anger is a part of the ancient fight-or-flight response, which evolved to help our survival. Just imagine a scenario that must have been relatively commonplace for our long-ago ancestors. We are peaceably minding our own business, cooking food over a fire or relaxing after a hard day's foraging or hunting, when a large, snorting wild animal leaps out from the thicket or you suddenly realise enemy tribesmen have crept into your village to raid it. We have to take *instant* action to protect ourselves. So, without us even having to think about it, our body immediately gets ready for extreme action:

- **Extra adrenalin is secreted into the bloodstream.** (Adrenalin is the hormone that gets us fired up and ready for action.)

- **Our breath comes faster,** to get oxygen into the bloodstream more quickly.

- **Our blood pressure goes up,** so that more blood reaches the muscles (enabling our legs to move faster) and the heart (which beats more rapidly in readiness for the extra demands that are going to be made on it).

- **Blood is diverted from organs such as the stomach, the liver and the intestines,** so that more can go to where it is needed right now – the heart, the muscles and the central nervous system. This means that our digestion is temporarily suspended (which explains why people who suffer from chronic anger often have problems with digestion).

- **Glucose is freed up to provide energy for action.**

- **Men experience a surge of testosterone,** the male sex hormone associated with aggression.

■ *Our bodies are flooded with the stress hormone cortisol to help all this to happen.* (When cortisol production is increased, the immune system doesn't work so well, explaining why chronic anger can leave us more susceptible to infections.)

In the fraction of a second all this takes, we are ready to take the necessary action – to flee from the wild animal or attack it with weapons; to run away as fast as possible from the enemy tribesmen or to stand our ground and fight them.

Whether we are angry or frightened – that is, whether we are ready to fight or to flee – our physiological reactions are similar. Either choice requires us to be able to move fast. We are aware of a surge of energy, a feeling of heat or cold, a pounding heart, quick breath, a desire to let out sound and an urge to move our limbs quickly and forcefully. But how we act on these feelings will differ according to whether we wish to fight or run away. When we feel fear, the energy surge is one of all-consuming terror: we may be in a cold sweat and want to scream, and the movements we want to make are those of running away. It is a bad set of feelings. When we feel strong anger, however, we feel empowered: we feel hot and excited, want to yell out loud and to use our limbs to make forceful contact with someone or something else.

Once we have taken action – fought or fled – we gradually calm down again. The high levels of stress hormones that have been flooding our bodies are either burned up by the action we took or dissipate as our bodies get back to normal functioning. This excellent system no doubt saved our ancestors' lives innumerable times when they faced such dangers daily. But it doesn't work so well today because far fewer of

Anger and sex

AS YOU may realise, we feel hot and excited and want to yell out and thrash our limbs about at other times too. At a physiological level, anger arousal is similar to sexual arousal. And, just as immediate anger is dissipated if physical action is taken, so sexual arousal is discharged by orgasm.

This close connection between anger arousal and sexual arousal explains why, as commonly happens, a couple can be having a furious row one minute and then be making mad, passionate love the next. Or why sexual frustration can tip over into physical violence: once an arousal has occurred, if it is thwarted sexually, the threshold is lowered for its expression through anger instead. In effect, if there is any kind of strong arousal, the stage is set and the transition from anger to sex, or sex to anger, occurs more readily.

The close connection between anger and sex also explains why some people can get addicted to anger, just as others get addicted to sex. Both enjoy the addictive 'high' which either activity can produce. ●

the challenges we encounter are of the sort that we can take immediate physical action to deal with. We can't berate our unreasonable boss, for instance, if we want to keep our jobs. And it's totally inappropriate for a mother to lash out when her son refuses to eat his specially cooked dinner. It is also not on

> **66** The first important tool for combating anger is information. **99**

for a driver to swear and gesticulate aggressively at another driver for taking 'his' parking spot or for an elderly man to be yelled at in annoyance by his adult children because he keeps repeating himself – yet this is what some people feel driven to do sometimes, if the accumulated stresses of the day have made them feel that they simply cannot cope with any more.

As we have seen, when we are gearing up for fight or flight, the body temporarily shuts down all its normal housekeeping functions and energy floods to our muscles, so that we can take action to save our lives. But if, instead of being temporary, this state of affairs continues because of ongoing, undischarged anger, it puts huge stress on the heart and also accounts for all those other health risks associated with anger, which were listed earlier.

What we need to do, therefore, is find healthier ways of discharging aroused anger – or preventing it from occurring inappropriately in the first place. We are going to present a lot of useful tools and strategies to help you do this, but the first important tool is – information. As the saying goes, forewarned is forearmed. Did you know, for instance, that, at certain times and in certain conditions, we are much more prone to anger outbursts than at others?

Conditions that lower the threshold for anger

Overtiredness: We tend to lose control of our emotions much more easily when we are tired. If we haven't had enough sleep, we are likely to become irritated much more quickly by anything that bothers us.

Ill health: If we are physically unwell in any way, we may lose control more easily because we feel so under par. Even little things can feel too much to cope with.

Hunger: Many people get grumpy and intolerant when they are hungry. But they often don't make the connection between the two events.

Cravings: People who are withdrawing from, or temporarily prevented from having, a substance they crave – such as nicotine, alcohol or drugs – can quickly become angry, and sometimes even violent, in situations that normally wouldn't bother them. In fact, the reason that many people use substances such or cigarettes or alcohol, or resort to comfort eating, in the first place, is to keep angry feelings in check. Having an anger outburst is a common reason for ex-smokers to relapse.

Hormonal changes: Hormonal swings experienced by women at times such as puberty, pre-menstruation, around childbirth and at the menopause may lead to exaggerated mood swings, including irritability and anger.

Chronic or acute pain: People who suffer chronic pain very often feel worn down by it. Understandably, this can cause them to have less tolerance of additional burdens or inconveniences and so they lose their tempers more readily.

Dementia: Those suffering from the early stages of dementia can quite often become angry quickly, as they struggle to cope

Why alcohol can make us aggressive

HAVING A few glasses of wine with friends or a few beers in the pub with good companions makes many people feel jolly, or mellow and more relaxed, and a pleasant time is usually had by all. Alcohol can even make us feel more loving and warm towards each other. So why then do accident and emergency departments fill up every night with people who have suffered injuries caused by someone becoming angry and violent whilst drunk? It seems paradoxical that a substance that can create such jovial good feeling can also cause violent anger and loathing. But the paradox disappears when you realise that what alcohol does is lower the threshold for emotional arousal *in general*. So, when things are going right, it may help us feel happy or lovey-dovey and sexy; but when we start to view things as going wrong or becoming annoying, it can just as easily trigger aggression instead.

with a frightening sense of loss of control. As their brain function deteriorates, the parts that normally keep anger impulses in check become impaired.

Any of the above causes will raise stress levels and lower the threshold for expressing anger.

Myths about anger

There are many mistaken beliefs about anger that often prevent people from dealing with it effectively. So, in case you were inadvertently influenced by any of them, let's dispel some of these before we go any further.

Myth 1 If you are angry, it is better to let it out

If you have anger inside you, so the mythology goes, it is best to let it rip. Even some therapists would tell you that this is a healthy thing to do. While no therapist would suggest, however, that you should beat someone up or shove your fist through doors, there was – and still is, in some quarters – quite a fashion for getting people to punch pillows, shout and fully express their anger. A typical scenario might be as follows. A woman goes to see a therapist because she is unhappy in her marriage. It quickly emerges that she has never stood up for herself and meekly accepts whatever her husband insists on, however miserable that makes her. She has ended up privately resentful, hostile and depressed. But she wants to make her marriage work again. The therapist decides that she needs to become more assertive and says she must "get in touch with her anger". He tells her to keep bashing a pillow as hard as she can, imagining it is her husband and yelling out all the feelings she has been unable to express: "I hate you, Kevin! You *never* listen to what I want to do! You never think about *my* needs. Where did all the romance go? I hate you!" etc.

By the end of it, she probably feels quite liberated and much calmer. The idea the well-intentioned but misguided therapist has is that she will return home re-energised, become more assertive in the future and also recover her former loving feelings towards her husband, now that all the anger has gone. This is the theory. But imagine for a moment two contestants in a world heavyweight boxing championship. They each spend the preceding weeks punching the hell out of a punchbag, encouraged to imagine that it is their opponent's head. If the 'let it out' theory were correct, by the time the day of the championship arrives, the two men would have no aggression left, and would want to hug each other instead!

Bashing pillows, or anything else, doesn't stop anger feelings from arising because it goes against an elementary rule in psychology: *whatever you practise, you become more skilled at.*

In dispelling the myths surrounding anger, we would like to acknowledge the groundbreaking and hugely influential work of the American social psychologist, Carol Tavris.

Think about it. If someone practises the piano regularly, they get better. If someone keeps making soufflé, they become proficient at it. The more we pronounce Spanish or French words correctly, the more authentic our accent becomes. The longer we spend practising yoga or martial arts or badminton or football, the better the technique we end up with. So, *if we practise anger, we get better at being angry.* That is why it is important not to let young children get away with having tantrums. If they learn that this is a good tactic to get what they want, they will use it at every opportunity.

> 66 If we continually express our anger – we only get better at being angry ... 99

When we practise something a lot, the nerve cells in our brains that are associated with that activity get strengthened. (When we stop doing something regularly, we often lose our special expertise in it, which is why there is the saying, "use it or lose it".)

So where did this misguided notion – that anger should be expressed, otherwise it is unhealthy – come from? It came about because there is a dangerous half-truth in it: When we express our anger, we lower our emotional arousal. After the pillow bashing, the wife definitely feels calmer. However, she only feels calmer at the *physiological* level – the stress hormones that were coursing round her body have been burned up. But, at another level, she has unknowingly set herself up for disaster. Just as with the piano playing, the soufflé making, the yoga exercise and so on, the more we practise anger, the more our brain cells connect up to respond in that way again and so the more readily anger will boil up in us in the future. Don't get what we want? Anger outburst. Don't like waiting in queues? Anger outburst. Resent our partner for not thinking to take off his muddy boots at the door? Anger outburst.

Worse, if we do get extremely angry and then re-run the scenario through our minds at another time, the same physiological effects occur – *even though we are just imagining it!* Californian researchers have found that, when couples are asked to recall an argument a week after it occurred, their blood pressure rises again. The researchers conclude that stressful events have the potential to continue to do harm long after they are over.* This makes complete sense, as we explain when we talk about patterns that reactivate anger, on page 30.

What we need to do, then, is find another way to lower arousal that doesn't involve anger and thus prevents us from 'getting good' at it. (We will look at several possible ways of doing this in Part 2.)

But surely talking out anger helps us get rid of it?

That all depends how you talk about it and with whom. Suppose John has a row with his wife, Kate. He thinks she is being totally unreasonable and is beginning to wish they had

---

* Glynn, L M, Christenfeld, N and Gerin, W (2007). Psychophysiology of anger. *International Journal of Psychophysiology*, 66, 2, 135–40.

never got married. He storms out to the pub where his mate Simon asks him what's wrong. John gives him a spirited account of what he sees as Kate's unreasonable demand that he give up one of the three nights that he goes out a week, two of which are spent on football training, so that he can stay in with the baby while she goes out with friends. Simon responds, "That's terrible! I think you should put your foot down and show her who's boss!" and much more in the same vein. After that conversation, and fuelled by a few beers, John is more likely to return home roused up and in a confrontational mood, rather than calmed down and in a conciliatory one.

No professional counsellor or therapist would respond that way, of course. One skill most counsellors are trained in is known as *active listening*, although we prefer the term *reflective listening*. This means the counsellor or therapist listens to what the aggrieved person has to say (without interrupting, being judgemental, offering an opinion or interspersing accounts of similar experiences from their own life) and then reflecting back to the client what they have been told by reiterating in their own words what they think they have heard, particularly the feelings being expressed, so that they can be sure they have understood them correctly.

Of course, when we are angry or upset with someone, we tend to dredge up every last thing that ever made us angry or upset about him or her. So reflective listening with John might go a bit like this:

"I see, so you feel that the three nights you go out every week are not really pleasurable because two of them involve hard football training, even though you do go to the pub afterwards, and so the third, when you go to the pub straight away, is your only real relaxing night out. You feel your wife doesn't appreciate that you're the breadwinner and you need to relax, and that Kate has never supported you in your love of football or appreciated the hard work you do to earn money, so that she can have the nice home she wants. Now you are thinking it was a mistake to get married."

> " ... there is a real risk that he will feel his angry views have been validated. "

Well, John will certainly feel heard, when all that is fed back to him, and that may well lower his emotional arousal. But there is a real risk that he will feel also that his angry views have been validated. After all, he has not been criticised for holding them, so by implication his therapist must approve of them (not necessarily the case at all, of course). The result may be that John will still think it is appropriate to get angry in a similar situation in the future. Even if the counsellor has helped John lower his arousal for the time being, he has not helped John find a better way to handle future confrontations with Kate. When counselling just consists of reflective listening like this it can actually wind people up and maintain them in their problematic state. This is because reflective (or active) listening *on its own* does not engage the client directly with problem solving or teach them about why people experience trouble with emotional responses.

Of course, talking out anger *can* sometimes be helpful, if we are also able to use the occasion to get our feelings under control and evaluate them more calmly. So it really does depend on the nature of the talk and the listener's ability to encourage self-questioning and reflection – which a good therapist will always do.

Myth 2 Suppressed anger causes depression

This is an incredibly common myth, often described thus: "Depression is anger turned inwards". However, a huge number of people in prison are depressed and a large proportion of prisoners are there because of violence of one kind or another – so they clearly have no trouble getting in touch with and expressing their anger. The truth is that depressed people are often extremely angry people, who feel they were dealt a dud hand in life or that nothing ever goes right for them, or that no one understands them. Although people who are depressed may seem flat and emotionless, they are actually highly emotionally aroused and have high levels of the stress hormone cortisol circulating in their blood. They are positively seething with emotion, including anger.

When people are depressed, they have low levels, unsurprisingly, of the 'feel good' hormone serotonin. (This is an effect of depression, not the cause.) And when serotonin levels are low, the experience of other negative emotions, such as anger and anxiety, is more likely.

There is one scenario in which suppressed anger may be a feature of depression, however. If someone who has used anger in the past to get their own way finds that that ploy no longer works for them – perhaps because their partner or colleagues refuse to put up with it anymore – they may well become depressed as a result. This is because they no longer know how to get their needs met. If they still get angry, they will most likely suppress it, because expressing it no longer delivers the goods. But the anger itself isn't the cause of their depression.

Myth 3 Women are not as aggressive as men

It is widely believed that women are the gentler sex and lack the aggression that is more common to men. But much research has been done which highlights that this is by no means always the case.

Although researchers have found that women are, on average, less assertive than men outside the home, within their own families, or with those close to them, they are just as likely as men to resort to aggression when they become uncontrollably angry. For instance, one major family violence study by the University of New Hampshire's Family Research Laboratory (conducted between 1975 and 1985 with a total of 8,145 married and cohabiting couples) showed that 12.4 per cent of women had assaulted their spouses, compared to 12.2 per cent of men. And when it came to severe assaults, the numbers were 4.6 per cent for women and 5 per cent for men. In 1999, a study by the British Home Office found that 4.2 per cent of men – the exact same figure as for women – had been assaulted by their partner in the previous year.

> **In the home, women and men get violent with roughly equal frequency ...**

Further research backs this up. Between 1997 and 2007 the Department of Psychology at California State University did a meta-analysis of 418 studies which conclusively found that women are as physically aggressive, or more aggressive, than men in their relationships with their spouses or male partners. (The aggregate sample size in the reviewed studies exceeded 201,500.)

And, surprising though it may seem, perpetrators of child abuse and/or neglect against children are more commonly women. A 1999 a report published by The Children's Bureau in America, Child Maltreatment 1999, found that "three-fifths (61.8%) of perpetrators of violence against children were female. The most common pattern of maltreatment was a child victimized by a female parent acting alone (44.7%)." Female parents were identified as the main perpetrators of neglect and physical abuse of child victims.

So, in the home, women and men get violent with roughly equal frequency. In one third of violent marriages, it is the man who gets violent; in another third, it's the woman; and in the final third, both are violent towards each other. (Domestic violence also occurs between gay couples.) The only big difference is that when it is men who are the violent ones they are more likely to do more physical damage to women than vice versa.

Myth 4 You can hold on to anger from childhood

We often hear people say something like, "I've got all this anger inside me, I've had it since childhood" or, "My anger has been building up for years!" They talk as if there is a well of anger somewhere inside them that just gets added to and added to until it can be contained no longer, and then it starts bursting out. Their excuse – or explanation – for behaving badly or inappropriately is that "it is all the anger coming out at last".

This is a notion that can be attributed to the father of psychoanalysis, Sigmund Freud, who first suggested that we hold on to the energy of unexpressed anger in our nervous systems. He was wrong. We now know absolutely that this isn't how the brain works.

Dreams deactivate unexpressed anger

Emotional arousal activates the instinctive arousal-discharge pattern in our autonomic nervous system (the part of the nervous system that controls the functions that aren't usually consciously directed, such as breathing, sweating etc.). This means that, once an emotion is experienced, it has to be discharged by our taking the relevant necessary action – such as fleeing or hiding when we feel fear or yelling or striking out when we feel anger (in just the same way as seeking food and eating puts an end to the instinctive feeling of hunger).

But, as we said earlier, we can't always act on our emotions – it might not be appropriate or possible. So, if there is any emotional arousal (or 'expectation') from the day that hasn't been expressed, and is therefore still present in the nervous system when we go to sleep, the brain will discharge it by acting it out in a dream that same night. (Completing the pattern that has been activated through metaphor in a dream brings the arousal levels back down.) This is nature's remarkably clever way of enabling us to start each day afresh, unencumbered by still active, unexpressed emotional arousal.*

---

* The discovery that it is *unexpressed emotional arousal* that gets expressed in dreams is known as the expectation fulfilment theory of dreaming and is fully explained in Griffin, J and Tyrrell, I (2004), *Dreaming Reality: How dreaming keeps us sane or drives us mad.* HG Publishing, East Sussex.

For instance, suppose Mike, the sales manager, is called in for a dressing down by his boss. The boss (not an emotionally intelligent man and probably under considerable stress himself to meet targets set by his own manager) is rude and insulting. He thumps the desk, calls Mike names and insists he improves sales immediately. Mike has to take all this without complaint, if he wants to keep his job. He comes out of his boss's office seething inside. All those fight-or-flight hormones are coursing around his body and he wants to 'punch his boss's head in'. As he goes home from work, he rehearses in his mind all the things he would like to say and do to his boss, sparing him no agony. Of course he wouldn't *do* any of them, even if he could, because he is a generally mild-mannered man. In fact, he probably won't even slam his car door to vent his feelings, nor tell his wife when he gets inside the house, as he doesn't believe in bringing his troubles home from work.

> 66 ... that night his unexpressed anger will be discharged in a dream. 99

When he goes to sleep that night, however, his unexpressed anger will be discharged in a dream, so that he can let it go. He won't dream about his boss directly because we always dream in metaphor.† Instead, he will unconsciously trawl his

---

† If we didn't dream in metaphor we would quickly lose the capacity to remain aware of the difference between waking reality and dreaming reality and create false memories. Dreaming in metaphor prevents our memory store from becoming either corrupt or incomplete. You can read more about the expectation fulfilment theory of dreaming and its implications at: www.why-we-dream.com

memory for an emotional connection to some other person who is or has been in authority over him – maybe a traffic warden or a headmaster – and vent his feelings on that person in the dream. If he remembers the dream (and we mostly don't, of course, because once the arousal has been discharged we have no need to, plus nature doesn't want us muddling up what is real with what was a dream), he might be a bit shocked to find he could have been quite so aggressive, even in a dream. The next day, he won't feel any warmer towards his boss, of course. But nor will he be experiencing the physical, emotional arousal and stress he felt the day before – unless something else happens to set it off once more. And if the boss does dish out yet another dose of criticism, making Mike feel impotent and angry all over again, he will dream out this new episode the following night. (He might even have the same dream, as nature is very economical.)

> 66 When we feel under threat, the fight-or-flight hormones come flooding through ... 99

All kinds of emotional expectations that we imagine but don't, or can't, act upon for whatever reason, are discharged through our dreams in this way, even the happy ones. (During the day we might have been looking forward to something positive, like a holiday, but, as it is in the future, the expectation cannot yet be fulfilled. This is just as powerful, in terms of undischarged expectations, as ruminating over something frustrating or annoying that has happened and can't now be changed.* Dreams, therefore, are not about suppressed wishes, as Freud supposed; they concern all expectations – positive or not – that have aroused us during the day but which were not fulfilled by taking action.) So the discovery about why we dream conclusively shows that we *don't* build up suppressed anger over months and years. We discharge it every night in our dreams and this helps keep us emotionally healthy – otherwise we would all be going around with a powder keg of anger inside, just waiting for a touch paper to set it off!

Dreaming out unexpressed anger also keeps the important instinct of anger intact. As we explained earlier, anger is a vital survival mechanism that we cannot afford to lose. But we would, if we kept suppressing it. If, for instance, we didn't have the emotional power to defend our sense of what is fair or just, or what is our due, we would let other people walk all over us. So, when we feel under threat, the fight-or-flight hormones come flooding through, making us ready to take action. But if we keep not taking action, because most of the time in a civilised society it is inappropriate to blow our tops, the instinct would start to fade – just as the urge to smoke or eat sweets eventually fades if we cease to give in to it. And then people *would* walk all over us! Dreaming out the angry

---

* These insights into why we dream have proved of tremendous importance in the understanding and treatment of depression. For more information, see: Griffin, J and Tyrrell, I (2004). *How to lift depression ... fast.* HG Publishing, East Sussex.

arousal at night fulfils the expectation that we are going to take action, and thus, by completing the pattern, keeps the instinct intact for whenever we may need it.

What we do hold on to are patterns that *reactivate* anger

While it is not true, therefore, that anyone can hold on to anger from childhood – or even from last year, last month or last week – it can certainly seem that way. This is because of a mental process we call 'pattern matching', which can reactivate anger and make it fresh. (This is exactly why recalling an argument a week later can get us worked up all over again and increase our blood pressure once more.)

Whenever we come across something new, we log it in our memories. Then, when we re-encounter it, we recognise it as familiar. We know a chair is a chair, for instance, and that it's for sitting on. We recognise a book and know it will have words and, perhaps, pictures inside. Using our memory and this pattern-matching process is how we make sense of the world without having to keep rediscovering it anew. It is what enables us to navigate our way through life, identifying whether the things we see, hear, touch, taste and smell in the course of it are things we need to worry about or not.

But it is a crude process. We recognise a chair as a chair, whether or not it has arms, upholstery or a straight or curved back. Similarly, we recognise a loud bang as threatening and jump – regardless of whether the source is a gunshot or a firework being let off. This is because the part of the brain most concerned with immediate pattern matching, a small organ called the amygdala, is not designed to be too specific. It is our brain's alarm system, designed to help keep us safe. (If it turns out there isn't an emergency, other parts of the brain can analyse the more subtle detail.)

The brain's alarm system

The amygdala has access to all our instinctive responses and also to our emotional memories, which are learned patterns that we consequently match to. It constantly scans the environment on the alert for any possible danger. If it makes a pattern match between what we are currently experiencing and our instincts or memories, it will make a split-second decision about whether we are at risk or not. It is the amygdala, by sounding the alarm, so to speak, that triggers the physiological events, described earlier, which set the fight-or-flight response in motion.

The amygdala is situated in what is often called 'the emotional brain'. (The 'thinking brain' – the neocortex – sits on top of it.) The emotional brain is concerned with our instinctive behaviours – responding to the urges to eat, drink, mate, sleep, fight, flee and so on. Animals just act on these urges, if it is safe to do so. On the whole, we humans, of course, use reason to temper our actions. We don't eat *every* cake we see, just because we experience a momentary desire for it; most sexual fantasies aren't acted upon; and, as we've said, we don't normally hit people if they irritate us by getting the last seat on the bus or train. So, when we hear a loud bang, we will jump and be on full alert but, if our thinking brain quickly realises that it is just a car backfiring or remembers it is bonfire night, or some other occasion celebrated with fireworks, we soon calm down again.

However, the important point we want to make here is that we respond (by jumping, in the above scenario), *before* the thinking brain gets a chance to check things out. This is because the amygdala actually gets the information half a second before the thinking brain does. That doesn't sound much but it can be crucial if we need to take instant action to save our life. However, because, as we said above, the amygdala's pattern matching is crude, it often gets things wrong (on the basis of 'better safe than sorry'). And this is what explains so many sudden outbursts of anger or violence.

Suppose Neil, who can be an angry man, discovers that his girlfriend, who has distinctive long, wavy, red hair, has been cheating on him. He is utterly shocked but, when he confronts her, she stands up to him, saying it is his fault because he works all hours and her new man is a much better lover. He is so hurt and enraged that, in the grip of his emotion, he lays into her, giving her a black eye and breaking two of her ribs. Afterwards, he is aghast at what he has done, but it is too late. Neil and his girlfriend split up acrimoniously (and he is lucky that she decides not to press charges).

Some time – perhaps years – later, he turns up at the doctor's surgery, feeling unwell with a bad cold that he

> 66 ... we respond *before* the thinking brain has a chance to check things out. 99

thinks has hung on too long, and is told there are no appointments. The receptionist telling him this, who is very firm and not that sympathetic, has long, wavy red hair. Before he knows what he is doing, he has punched her in the face. Afterwards, he is shocked and horrified. He can't understand his action. But he did what he did because he had subconsciously pattern matched back to a similar situation, where he was highly emotional and felt he was being unjustly treated. His amygdala had made an instantaneous association between threat and confrontation with a young woman with long red hair.

The thinking brain and the amygdala can't be in charge at the same time. So, if the amygdala is on high red alert, it doesn't let the thinking brain get a look in at all. At the moment when Neil lands his punch, he won't be thinking for one second that this is the wrong thing to do ... because he won't be thinking at all!

Anger makes us 'stupid'

Even if we don't act on the 'threat' that the amygdala has perceived, and don't take flight or fight, the very act of pattern matching to the 'threat' results in a cascade of signals being sent up to the thinking brain – which we experience as emotional arousal. This has an adverse effect on the way that the thinking brain can process information, leaving it working under par. On top of this, the emotional arousal can continue for a long time after the original event that roused us up occurred and, the more emotionally aroused we are, the less able the thinking brain is to take in new information, analyse situations, make correct judgements and so forth.

> 66 The thinking brain and the emotional brain can't be in charge at the same time. 99

It is as if the amygdala has at its disposal an on/off switch and a dimmer switch: it can shut off the thinking brain completely, while it gears up for flight or fight (that's a good thing, temporarily, as we can't be standing around evaluating options, when someone is brandishing a knife or a car is hurtling towards us); or it can lessen our thinking power and stop the brain from functioning properly for quite some time, which isn't such a good thing at all.

In other words, high emotional arousal of any kind – not

just anger but anxiety, depression, greed, sexual desire etc. – makes us temporarily stupid.

Black-and-white thinking

By the very nature of its role, the amygdala can only 'think' in black or white. This is because, when it feels under threat, there are only two things it is interested in: "Do I fight or do I flee?"

When we are emotionally aroused and in black-and-white thinking mode, we aren't open to other people's viewpoints and we can't see a wider picture. Either we are right or we are wrong – and we are *definitely* not wrong! We have probably all had this sort of experience. Say your partner can't find the car keys. You tell him or her that you put them in the usual place. Your partner says, "Well, they aren't there. You must have put them somewhere else."

"I never put them anywhere else," you say huffily.

"You used the car last. You must have."

You are starting to get riled. "I *didn't* put them in a different place! You must have picked them up just now and then gone and done something else before going out. And now you can't remember where you put them down!"

"I didn't do anything beforehand."

By now you are getting extremely heated. "You **must** have! You're always losing keys. You never think where you put things. I put them back on the rack."

"You couldn't have!"

"I did! I did! I know I did! I can even see myself now, coming in from taking the dog to the park, and putting them back on the rack!"

"Oh yes, of course..." says your partner. "You took the dog in the car to the park for his walk! Didn't you rush into the kitchen to get a cloth from the cupboard under the sink, so that you could wipe his feet before he went on the carpet? Oh, look! Here are the keys, on the floor by the door of the cupboard under the sink!"

In such circumstances, we are stunned to find that we were wrong because, in our high state of arousal, we were totally convinced we were right.

Because people are in the grip of such blinkered, black-and-white thinking when they are highly emotionally aroused, one of the most ineffective – and possibly dangerous – responses to someone else's anger is to argue with them. The amygdala of an angry person is already excited. If it gets more excited still, perceiving more 'threat' in the situation, the result could well be physical violence.

It is also absolutely pointless to get into an argument about the 'truth' of a situation. Imagine you are arguing passionately for some viewpoint you hold whilst someone else is arguing just as heatedly against you for theirs, which is the total opposite. Suddenly, they stop and declare, "Goodness, you're right! How could I have been so stupid? Thank you so much for pointing out my error of judgement." Well, that would be news indeed! It never happens, of course. When we are emotionally aroused, we can see only our own viewpoint or interpretation of a situation. Truth is relative and what each of us proposes from our own individual perspective is not likely to be a rounded view. Far better to avoid such thankless arguments in the first place, as they can so often escalate into anger and violence.

There are plenty of other examples of black-and-white thinking that can stoke up anger, which will then either stay churning around inside you, causing stress, or else may lead to aggression. Here are a few of them:

■ *Jumping to conclusions*

"Anyone who does that is an absolute fool!"

"That driver cut me up deliberately!"

"You think you're so clever, don't you?"

■ *Blaming others*

"Now look what you've made me do!"

"The collision was her fault for slowing down when I was right behind her."

■ *Sweeping generalisations*

"All judges (doctors/bus drivers/people over 50) are idiots."

"That never used to happen in the old days."

"He's wearing a hoodie. He must be up to no good."

"Everyone's got it in for me."

"All Germans are Nazis."

■ *Taking a position*

"It's always wrong to tell a lie."

"My country, right or wrong."

"There's no such thing as a mistake."

■ *Exaggerating reactions*

"If she doesn't give me a pay raise, I'm going to kill her."

Black-and-white thinking of this kind just increases your likelihood of suffering chronic anger, with its accompanying continual low-level arousal and health risks.

'Anger management' is only half the answer

Perhaps, at some time in the past, you have taken or been referred to an anger management course. These are, as the name implies, courses that help you identify triggers for your anger, teach skills and techniques to help you handle it and, perhaps, change the way you think about certain things, so that they stop making you so angry. Some of these techniques, we are sure, you have found very useful. However, such courses leave out a crucial understanding. All people, including children, only suffer from excessive anger if something is not working in their lives. Only if we can find out what it is that is missing or malfunctioning can we learn how to get our lives back on track and have a *real* chance of making long-lasting changes. That is what the human givens approach is all about.

The human givens

Every one of us is born with innate needs that must be met for us to be physically and mentally healthy. There is wide agreement about what these needs are and they, together with the resources we have been given by nature to help us meet them, are what we call the 'human givens' – the givens of human nature. When our innate needs are being met in healthy ways, we are able to live balanced, fulfilled lives. It is only when they are not being met, or are not met healthily or in balance, that we start to become distressed and show signs of mental ill health, such as anxiety, depression or inappropriate anger.

We need to be motivated to take the actions that will help us get our innate needs met and that is the job of our emotions. Just as the feeling of hunger evolved in us so that we would search for food and eat, so feelings of pleasure but also frustration, anxiety, boredom, anger, depression etc. drive us to try to get specific unfulfilled needs met.

If we take a moment to look at each important need individually, we can see why anger and aggression might result from their being unmet.

Our physical needs

We all need warmth, shelter, sufficient sleep, food and drink. And what we eat is particularly important in relation to anger control because different foods, and certain colouring and preservative additives found in a variety of foods and drinks, are known to affect brain chemistry in different ways. For instance, certain foods can make children and even some adults highly emotionally aroused and hyperactive, and can generate temper tantrums, while other foods help calm them down (see page 97).

Our emotional needs

Decades of health and social research have shown that having particular emotional needs met is essential. The main ones are:

■ *Security – a sense of being safe, which enables us to lead our lives without undue fear*
All animals need to feel safe. If you feel continually or constantly under physical threat of assault, perhaps because of

where you live or who you live with, this is going to be a major cause of stress. Very commonly, too, abuse begets abuse. A recent large-scale study carried out at the National Center for Injury Prevention and Control in Atlanta has found that those who were neglected or physically abused in childhood are more likely to be violent in adolescence than unharm-

> **66 Many adults and children lash out against others when they feel unsafe and insecure ... 99**

ed children, and that those who were violent in adolescence are more likely to be violent to a partner in adulthood. Women who have been neglected or physically abused in childhood are more likely to be violent to partners as adults, regardless of whether they were violent as adolescents. Both men and women who were sexually abused as children are more likely to be violent in adolescence, according to the findings.*

For some people – adults and children alike – it is when they feel most unsafe and insecure that they lash out against others, as a means of protecting themselves (just as some animals will do when cornered).

---

* Fang, X and Corso, P S (2007). Child maltreatment, youth violence, and intimate partner violence: developmental relationships. *American Journal of Preventive Medicine*, 33, 4, 281–90.

■ *A sense of autonomy and control over our lives*

If major decisions that affect us are made without our being involved or consulted – for instance, job reorganisation, redundancy, financial decisions, moving house – we quickly feel powerless and out of control. Almost any unwanted situation can do it: an inconsiderate neighbour keeping us from sleeping night after night; being caught up in an unexpected traffic jam; being forced to tangle with bureaucracy or suddenly becoming seriously unwell, causing our body not to respond as it should.

■ *Attention – receiving it from others, but also giving it*

We all need to give and receive attention in balance but, for some people who have been deprived of it in childhood, it can be like a drug. They will do anything to get attention, even if it is negative attention. This is why many children behave extremely badly. As they commonly don't get given attention when they are good, or if more attention is paid to a younger, more needy sibling, they will misbehave, and perhaps have temper tantrums, just to ensure they get the attention they need.

■ *Emotional connection to other people – friendship, love, intimacy, fun*

People who have been emotionally or physically abused as children are very often too scared to allow the closeness of an intimate relationship, in case they are hurt again. Because they don't feel good about themselves, they may fear losing any partner they develop a relationship with and so, to protect against that, become jealous, over-controlling and often violent.

■ Connection to the wider community – being part of a larger group

We are social animals and need to feel that we 'belong'. This stems back to our ancient past when we could not survive on our own because predators would attack and eat us. Our survival always depended on being part of a large, noisy group and if we were ejected from the group it meant almost certain death at the fangs of some wild beast. Today, gang culture is rife in places where young people don't feel accepted as part of their wider community and so establish one of their own instead, where they can set the rules themselves and impose the penalties (thus also meeting their needs for autonomy and status). However, an excessive need to belong, whether to a gang or a particular cult or religion, can also generate prejudice and a sense of 'them' versus 'us', which in turn can lead to violence.

> 66 It is only when our innate needs are not being met that we start to show distress ... 99

■ *Privacy – to reflect on, and consolidate, experience*

It is well known from studies of many animal species, including our own, that overcrowding leads to conflict. Not everyone can have their own personal space, such as their own bedroom or study, den or potting shed, but we all need to be able to find somewhere to be alone sometimes, when we wish to be. People who are prone to anger particularly need time alone to calm down (see page 129).

■ *A sense of status – being accepted and valued in the different social groups we belong to*

Most of us play different roles in different areas of our lives – for instance, someone could be a parent, a sibling, a colleague, a friend and an amateur golfer, among other things – and this usually brings us enough status to feel that we 'count'. But, as mentioned, some of those who don't feel valued by the wider society may drop out of it and establish their own groups, in which this need for status will be met. A gang leader or a drug dealer, for example, has a status that is denied them elsewhere. And such 'underworld' status may have to be maintained through violent means.

■ *A sense of our own competence and achievement*

The brain needs to be kept busy. It evolved to develop the skills required to meet our needs and it rewards us with good feelings when we do. Knowing we are competent and have a history of worthwhile achievements in at least some areas of life protects us from developing low self-esteem. Feeling 'like rubbish' can often manifest in aggression and anger outbursts. For instance, a teenager who finds school work too hard or who struggles to read or write properly may resort to hurling a chair across the classroom and declaring that the task is stupid, rather than be exposed in front of their class as incompetent. (The way to dissolve feelings of being useless is to demonstrate to such a person that they can learn and achieve.)

> **" Feeling frustrated or that things are pointless can trigger anger outbursts ... "**

■ *A sense of meaning and purpose – which comes from doing things that mentally and/or physically stretch us*
When what we are doing lacks meaning or seems pointless, we feel frustrated and anxious, and may well become depressed. Feeling frustrated or that things are pointless can also trigger anger outbursts. In contrast, when we *are* being healthily stretched, life is intrinsically meaningful. The three main sources of meaning for us are: serving others (as in raising a family, teaching, nursing, providing employment); learning and perfecting skills or understanding (as in sport, the arts, intellectual endeavours, science, professional development); and being connected

to a belief system that extends way beyond our immediate daily concerns (as in a philosophical, political, social, religious or spiritual sense).

Our innate resources

Every species on earth, every living thing, whether a sunflower, a worm, gorilla or human being, inherits a genetic blueprint to help it get its needs met – we can think of it as an innate 'guidance system', which includes a wealth of resources, or a set of 'guidelines' that directs it towards the nourishment it needs to thrive. When these resources are not used properly or are damaged – which can happen for a variety of reasons – the life form cannot thrive.

We humans are born with a wealth of innate resources. They include:

- *the ability to add new knowledge to innate knowledge: to learn from experience and remember*

- *the ability to build rapport, empathise and connect with others*

- *emotions and instincts*

- *a powerful imagination, to aid problem solving*

- *the ability to think things out, analyse, plan and adapt*

- *the ability to understand the world unconsciously – through the process we call pattern matching*

- *the ability to step back into our 'observing self'
  (our self-awareness) – and be more objective*

- *the ability to dream and thus discharge any unexpressed
  emotionally arousing expectations, so that we can face each
  day afresh.*

In Part 2, we will be looking at how we can make the most effective use of these resources to help ourselves deal with anger.

What prevents people from flourishing

At a fundamental level, there are just three reasons that can prevent us from getting our emotional needs met. One or more of these three factors are what ultimately cause all forms of suffering and are at the root of all mental ill health, including anger disorders.

1. The environment is unhealthy

The family unit itself may be unhealthy. Children who are physically or verbally abused at home clearly can't get many of their essential needs met there; they may grow up dysfunctional and be physically or verbally abusive to others. Other unsafe and unhealthy environments include schools or workplaces where people are not stretched in healthy ways, or where bullying is experienced, or where peer group pressure to join in destructive behaviour (such as binge drinking or antisocial violent behaviour), arises. Poor living conditions and institutions such as care homes for young people or old people's homes where there is little positive stimulation are unhealthy too. Others find living in our lop-sided, materialistic, greed-based society unhealthy and amoral. Many feel that they are drowning in a sea of gadgets and information, with no real meaning, or are perpetually frustrated by a growing lack of autonomy and control that myriad new laws and more and more bureaucracy are bringing us. Even a long daily commute to work, driving in heavy traffic or on a crowded train, can increase stress levels. Unless one escapes or protects oneself in some way from an unhealthy environment, the stress it generates will eventually express itself through increased frustration and anger outbursts or in one of several other ways – perhaps an anxiety disorder, depression, addiction, psychotic breakdown or physical illness – any one of which can also result in anger outbursts.

2. The innate guidance system is damaged (temporarily or permanently)

This can come about because of genetic faults affecting the brain and therefore behaviour (as in autism) or direct physical damage, caused by a head injury, for instance. More often, however, the damage is psychological: it is caused by trauma. When psychological trauma occurs, the brain may continue pattern matching to occasions that were threatening in the past just as if they are still threatening in the present. When people suffer from post-traumatic stress disorder (PTSD), which can occur for any number of reasons (such as being mugged, surviving fire or drowning, experiencing a train or car crash), they can become explosively angry very quickly, as a result of their ongoing high levels of stress.

Addictions and obsessions, too, can corrupt the way the innate guidance system works, substituting life-enhancing drives for destructive impulses.

3. The innate guidance system isn't being used properly

We come into the world as helpless babies and, to ensure we thrive, our parents and other responsible older children and adults have to take care of our every need. Gradually, however, we must all learn for ourselves how to operate and survive in the world. Spreading outwards from the strong root of a loving, healthy family, our social network grows. The innate human abilities nature programmed us with – to be sociable, to share, to delay gratification, to build relationships and understand what others are feeling so we can take their feelings and needs into account as well as our own – are enriched. We learn, use information, make judgements, prac-tise skills, build careers and create meaningful lifestyles and – if all goes well – mature into rounded individuals. But, for

> **Our imagination can cause us huge problems if we misuse it.**

many reasons and often through no fault of their own, this does not happen for everyone.

Some parents don't know how to create the rich experiential environment that children need. If they lack fundamental life skills themselves, they cannot pass them on. They might condition their offspring in learned helplessness or that it's not worth bothering to make an effort, or that material possessions will make people happy. If our parents are unloving, we don't learn to trust people easily; if they are over-protective, we are made anxious about exploring and taking risks. If we are humiliated in the home or when we make mistakes at school or at work, we can fail to develop confidence in ourselves as effective human beings. (Fortunately, with the right help, all this can be redressed.)

Sometimes, we unwittingly use aspects of our internal guidance system incorrectly. Our imagination, for instance, is a powerful aid in problem solving, but it can also cause problems itself, if misused. Many people, for example, wind themselves up and get highly emotionally aroused by bringing to mind slights that they have received in the past, or fear they might receive in the future, or by running angry scenarios through their minds; others can make themselves anxious or depressed by imagining all kinds of catastrophic or miserable outcomes for themselves.

Reasons for excessive anger

Inappropriate anger responses can all be accounted for by one of the three scenarios just described. So now let's look in more detail at the reasons that excessive anger occurs.

Anger resulting from a build up of stress

If you have too many demands being made on you and/or you don't feel on top of your circumstances, you are likely to suffer from feelings of stress. Negative feelings like this are signals that something isn't working in our lives. Stress, therefore, is what we feel when the pressures and demands on us build up to such an extent that they are interfering with our ability to get our innate emotional needs met and, for whatever reason, we feel incapable of doing anything about it (which further depletes our sense of autonomy and control).

This means that those stress hormones that we described earlier are constantly circulating in your body and they need to get out! So, if something happens, big or little, that feels like 'the final straw', that's when you may blow. You might even feel better for a while, because at least your anger discharges all that pent up energy, but then probably remorse kicks in. After all, your kids didn't deserve quite such an earful, just because one of them accidentally knocked over a glass; and your colleague was only doing his or her best, even though they got something wrong; and you certainly regret throwing that fork at your partner, when he or she commented that the vegetables were a bit overcooked.

When we are over-stressed like this, we have little control over our emotions; we can't think straight because we are in such a high state of emotional arousal. (It's because this arousal turns off our intelligence for a while that people can benefit from the help of a good therapist. If your own brain isn't working well you can, in effect, borrow someone else's to help you until you can think straight again.) The important thing, then, is to take a realistic look at your circumstances and, if your anger outbursts are getting uncomfortably regular and threatening your relationships, your job and/or your health, you need to make some changes. (We will be looking at this in depth in Part 2.)

Irene came to see Ivan because she had become angry and abusive towards her husband. It was totally out of character for her and she was upset by, although seemingly powerless to change, her behaviour. It had all started after Irene had had a hysterectomy. The operation had gone wrong and left her unable to control her bladder and in permanent pain. It was not surprising that she felt angry so much of the time: she was incredibly frustrated that she could no longer do the job she had formerly loved, had lost all confidence and never felt physically well. As a result, she felt so bad about herself, that she had withdrawn from her friends (having also flared up at many of them) and the activities she had once enjoyed so much. Ivan was able to show her effective ways to manage her pain so that it could be less engulfing, which reduced her frustration. He also got her to concentrate on her appearance again (she'd always loved to have her hair and clothes looking good), to return to hobbies and social activities with friends and to go out for meals and to the cinema with her husband, as she had used to. Soon, she discovered for herself that, if important needs were met, she could cope better with her pain and she no longer needed to feel so angry all the time.

Anger and lack of negotiation skills

As very young children, we think the world revolves around us; we are the centre of the known universe and should automatically get everything we want. In a healthy family we soon learn that life doesn't work that way, but whether we then find out how to negotiate for what we want depends on how well we were taught as children and what we learned from our carers' way of doing things. Someone whose father or mother got their way by physical force or emotional blackmail, for example, is quite likely to grow up thinking that those are acceptable ways of getting their needs met. For relationships at home and at work to be fruitful and satisfying for all involved in them, we need to know how to give and take, when to take responsibility and make compromises and how to set up win–win situations, where possible.

> 66 It isn't difficult to learn the skills of negotiation and compromise ... 99

Passive aggression is another common way that lack of communication and negotiation skills may manifest. People who are passive-aggressive give no indication, at the time, that they are unhappy with a situation. The passive-aggressive husband or wife, girlfriend or boyfriend, apparently willingly agrees to their partner's choice of film; the passive-aggressive employee does not complain one jot when asked to take on extra tasks, and so on. They give no overt sign that they would rather see another film or can't handle the extra work. Instead, they find other ways of demonstrating their displeasure. They may stockpile their grievances, saving them all up until months later, when they burst out with them all at once. Or they may sulk, hardly talk, be constantly mildly disdainful or give someone the cold shoulder, without ever explaining why. They may even spread complaining, malicious gossip to others, use headaches or claims of illness to get their own way, or find other ways to sabotage plans, such as being late, 'forgetting' to do things they have agreed to do or unexpectedly doing things without telling their partner what they have surreptitiously planned. People who use passive-aggressive tactics a lot have not learned how to be up front about their own needs and wants.

It is not difficult to learn the skills of negotiation and compromise, however late in life, and it can have a dramatically positive impact on personal relationships. We explain them in Part 2.

Anger and chronic low self-esteem

When someone has been made to feel that they are 'worthless' and are said to suffer from chronic low self-esteem, they have permanently low levels of the feel-good brain chemical serotonin, the effect being to leave them without any emotional 'brakes'. As a result, they get fired up very quickly about anything they perceive as a slight – and, because they are insecure, they find slights where no one else could possibly imagine them.

Pathologically jealous people who are violent towards their partners usually have extremely low self-esteem. Perhaps their partners are vivacious and attractive, but they themselves feel – deep down – that they aren't and so have no chance of keeping the interest of their boyfriend or girlfriend, husband or wife. They are permanently worried that they will lose their partner and play out fantasies in their minds in which their man/woman betrays them (thus misusing their imaginations to make themselves feel even more powerless). Often they may make cruel remarks to put their partner

Why some women stay with violent partners

IT MAY seem amazing that a woman can stay with a partner who is consistently violent towards her – and even profess strong love for him and speak out in his defence. Or perhaps you *are* that woman. Pat Wallace, an independent domestic violence consultant and trainer for an organisation called Breaking Free, suggests that such behaviour by the victims of domestic violence may be a form of Stockholm syndrome.*

The term Stockholm syndrome was first coined in 1973, when three women and a man, who had been held hostage for several days by bank robbers in Stockholm, unexpectedly showed support and sympathy for their captors after the latter's arrest, even to the extent of raising money for their defence and visiting them in prison. The syndrome describes the seemingly inexplicable bonding that can occur between captive and captor when victims think their lives are at risk, believe they can't escape, are isolated from any perspective other than the captor's and even see the captor as kind – perhaps for giving them food or just allowing them to live.

Wallace suggests that these conditions also apply in a domestic violence context. First, the perpetrator makes his partner believe that she is at his mercy by being physically abusive towards her or other family members, causing damage to property or threatening to kill himself or her if she leaves. Second, the woman may feel that she is trapped, even if physically she is not, perhaps because she believes that she can't manage on her own financially or that she will be harmed or her children will be kept from her if she goes. Third, the abuser may stop her ▷

down, in the hope of making them feel worthless and that they are unlikely, if they leave, to attract another mate.

This is what had happened to Marie, a young woman who once sought Joe's help. A few years previously, she had become pregnant in her teens and, terrified of her parents'

from going out alone or prevent her from seeing family or friends, or from using the phone, thus inducing isolation. She may start to believe him when he says, "This happens in all relationships". As she is expecting to be killed in violent temper, little kindnesses such as his being friendlier or not beating her are taken as signs that he is 'not all bad'. Hoping that this is a sign that things are improving, the woman may deny her fear and concentrate on the positives she sees in her abusive partner.

An abused woman living in such a situation, Wallace suggests, feels an overwhelming need to pacify her abuser – becoming docile and dependent and keen to attend to all of his wants, for example through sex and good cooking; she adopts his world view, feels grateful to him and rejects offers of help, which she fears may annoy her 'captor'.

Of course, it is well known that men can also be the victims of domestic violence, so if the above paragraphs have described your situation (whether you are male or female), then, for the sake of your safety and sanity, and that of anyone else at risk in the family, please get out or get help. ●

*Wallace, P (2007). How can she still love him? Domestic violence and the Stockholm Syndrome. *Community Practitioner*, 80, 10, 32–34. For more information about Breaking Free, visit http://myweb.tiscali.co.uk/breakingfree

disapproval, had believed her boyfriend when he told her that she was an embarrassment to her family and that she had better give up her plans to go to university and come to live with him instead, because only he would want to care for her and the baby. Soon afterwards, however, she discovered that he was frighteningly over-controlling. He wouldn't let her see her parents or her friends; if she bought some little thing for their home without consulting him, he would stamp on it and break it; worst, when she had her baby girl, he started to shake her to stop her crying. Realising her daughter's life was truly in danger, she managed to break out of her thrall of fear and escape from their flat when her partner wasn't there. She then fled home to her family, who welcomed her with open arms, and helped her get back on track with her studies, as well as assisting with the baby. However, the trauma of this experience later had an effect on her ability to maintain new relationships with boyfriends, which was why she ended up seeking help from Joe.

Chronic low self-esteem tends to develop as a result of long-term physical or emotional abuse like this. If you are told throughout your childhood, for example, that you're useless and will never amount to anything, such relentless 'brain-washing' takes a hold. It may become impossible for the victim of such abuse to believe in themselves or feel any sense of value. Whatever they achieve, they may find themselves pattern matching back to those painful taunts of "You're rubbish! Everyone hates you!" and, as a result, denigrating their achievements or even sabotaging them. So the student who is doing well in a subject fails to turn up to take the exam or the promising employee decides not to take up the offered promotion.

Thankfully for anyone struggling like this, there is effective help available in the form of a simple, non-invasive technique (commonly known as the 'rewind technique' – see page 197) which can be used to stop these unhelpful pattern matches. Skilled professionals trained in using it can, in most cases, successfully neutralise such painful memories (sometimes even years of trauma) in a couple of therapy sessions. They then concentrate on helping the individual to build up relationship skills and increase their confidence in themselves.

Anger and the autistic spectrum

More people nowadays are diagnosed as being on the autistic spectrum – which covers a range of brain differences from full-blown autism and Asperger's syndrome (a high functioning form of autism) through to much lesser autistic traits, such as being more interested in and comfortable with technology than people. All sufferers from autism, severe or mild, have marked difficulties in relating to other people and commonly experience huge frustration generally, which can trigger violent anger outbursts. Autistic rage is terrible to behold: so untamed as to often be described as "demonic". But those with Asperger's syndrome don't necessarily immediately stand out, especially if they are female. However, they all experience the world differently from most people – they are 'straight-line thinkers', are often seen as eccentric, can become intensely taken up by one particular interest area, to the point of obsession (thus forgetting commitments and responsibilities), and, because of a more limited social understanding and ability to relate, find it harder to engage with people in the usual sorts of ways.

> **"... intense frustration and anger outbursts can result if something unexpected happens ... ""**

Many people meet and are attracted to each other without either of them realising that one partner has Asperger's syndrome. Eccentricities may come across to the other partner as thoughtlessness or a lack of caring (failure to turn up to arrangements, for instance, or not phoning when they've agree to do so) and, understandably, can thus cause considerable relationship difficulties.

People with Asperger's syndrome tend to feel a need for ritual and rigid order and so they like to control things. If they are in relationships, they may well come across as 'control freaks', who insist on everything being done as *they* want it done. This can result in intense frustration and outbursts of anger, if something unexpected happens that prevents them from getting their way. Because people with Asperger's syndrome are also highly sensitive to sensory overload (often finding it difficult to cope with noise levels or bright lighting that doesn't bother others), and because they are often very uncomfortable in unfamiliar places, they may lose their tempers easily in such circumstances.

Once the syndrome has been identified, however, couples and families can be helped to find ways to manage and minimise the difficulties such behaviours can cause. If you suspect that either you or your partner, or someone else you know, may suffer from Asperger's syndrome, you or they might like to take the Autism Spectrum Quotient test.*

Anger and brain damage

Often the people who end up as violent criminals are those who, as young children, repeatedly suffered beatings to the body and head from those supposedly caring for them. Not only may they have been traumatised by what they suffered but many are also likely to suffer some irreparable brain damage that prevents them from having full control over their impulses.

Other kinds of brain damage can also affect the areas of the brain concerned with impulse control. Head injuries caused in

---

*You can find this test in *The Essential Difference: men, women and the extreme male brain* (Allen Lane, 2003) by Simon Baron-Cohen, a leading expert on autistic spectrum disorders. (A similar test is also available online at: www.autismresearchcentre.com)

accidents and damage to the brain caused by stroke or dementia may all result in aggressive behaviour that is completely out of character with the sufferer's previous personality.

Anger and addiction

Drug addicts, as we know, may be so desperate for their next fix that they will resort to anything to get it, including violence. But it isn't just substances that people get addicted to. We can get addicted to anything that seems to give us a 'high' – whether it is sex, exercise, shopping or anger outbursts.

Addiction hijacks our internal 'reward' system which nature developed to help us learn and strive for new experiences. When we are getting our innate needs met in balance, and in healthy ways, there is no room for addictive behaviour. Anyone who has to engage compulsively in any one particular activity, especially when it damages themselves or others, cannot be getting their needs met in a healthy, balanced way. Being engaged fully with life, aiming for and achieving goals, feeling life is meaningful – these bring natural, fulfilling highs. Addictive behaviour, on the other hand, brings fake highs that don't last long, quickly become less satisfying and tend to have to be repeated more and more often, to attain ever-diminishing returns.

> 66 We can get addicted to anything that gives us a 'high' – and that includes anger outbursts. 99

The drinker may need to drink more. The person who gets an 'anger high' may become increasingly violent.

People who enjoy getting angry are maintaining themselves in a highly aroused state. That means that they are trapped into black-and-white thinking and, as we have seen, the result is a false sense of clarity and righteousness. They also tend to think that they have a right to their anger and damn the consequences for anyone else – this is clearly addictive thinking. To break the pattern, they need to be helped to see that the 'highs' of their anger outbursts are not worth the very real risks – such as failed relationships, broken families, spells in jail, heart disease and early death.*

Anger triggered by fear

Denny was given a life sentence for murder when he battered his friend to death on a freezing cold night for no reason that he could articulate. He and his best friend Nick were 'down and out'. Having failed to get the jobs that they had travelled to a distant city in search of, they had then both hitchhiked and trudged, cold and hungry, the 90 miles back to their home town. On arrival, they huddled in a derelict building, desperately burning any wood they could tear down to make fires

---

*You will find plenty of help on overcoming any kind of additive behaviour in *Freedom from Addiction: the secret behind successful addiction busting* by Joe Griffin and Ivan Tyrrell (HG Publishing, 2005).

for warmth. Quite reasonably, Nick suggested that they go to Denny's mother's house, as it was only 500 yards away, and sleep on her front room floor. But Denny wouldn't hear of it. And when he ran out of arguments against Nick's pleadings, Denny battered him to death.

But *why*? They were good mates. Nick hadn't threatened him. All Denny could say in explanation afterwards was, "I just went too far". Denny had absolutely no idea why he had felt compelled to kill his best friend, only that the 'need' was overwhelming. It finally emerged, through the work that psychiatrist Dr Bob Johnson subsequently carried out with Denny in Parkhurst Prison, that Denny had been driven to murder because he was still frozen in a state of terror of his mother, who had battered him cruelly as a boy. The fear wasn't conscious. Nor was it rational. He was, after all, now an adult and a strapping six feet three and a half inches tall at that, while she was 85 and just five feet two.*

This case is an example of pattern matching that had extreme and serious consequences. Denny had been so traumatised as a boy by his treatment at his mother's hands that panic welled up uncontrollably at what was, to him, the intolerable prospect of being hurt by her again. The pattern match caused such fear in him that he could only control the situation through violence.

---

* Johnson, B (1997). Narrative approaches with lifers. *The Therapist*, 4, 3, 24–28.

Denny is not alone – anger is a common reaction to fear and humiliation. An individual who has pattern matched to some traumatic event in their past may well do anything to avoid experiencing such powerlessness and pain again. In effect, they lash out in terror or fight to protect themselves against what feels to them like a very real current threat, instead of one that is in the past. That is what a post-traumatic stress reaction does: it makes a terrifying situation from the past feel as if it is happening all over again in the present.

> **" Denny had absolutely no idea why he had felt compelled to kill his best friend. "**

Sometimes, as in Denny's case, the cause of the pattern match is not immediately apparent. Pattern matching always happens at an unconscious level and is virtually instantaneous, but often the source can be quickly recognised. A woman, for instance, who has escaped from a relationship in which she was abused may lash out in un-provoked anger at a new partner, however kind and caring, if he happens to say something or wear something that brings back a memory of a terrifying occasion with the former, abusive partner. She may be well aware almost immediately of the reason for her reaction but that doesn't prevent her angry outburst. This is exactly what was happening to Joe's client Marie, who had escaped with her baby daughter from her abusive partner. When she later met a young man whom she loved very much and who was very kind and loving to both her and her daughter, she would frequently lash out against him in anger.

Fortunately, Joe was soon able to help Marie and she and her partner were able to settle down to their new life together. As we have already mentioned, effective therapists can quickly stop people from pattern matching to the past like this by using the rewind detraumatisation technique (see page 197). However, if abuse is ongoing, the technique cannot work (as new traumas will be occurring) so steps have to be taken to deal with the current problem first – such as leaving the abusive partner or getting help for them.

Irrational anger, triggered by a hidden cause

Most of us have experienced losing our cool or blowing our tops over something quite ridiculous at one time or another. Sometimes it happens because a build up of stresses has worn down our reserves of energy, so that when some relatively minor mishap occurs, it feels like the final straw and, to the astonishment of those around us, we erupt. But more often than not, we just cannot understand what caused us to react in such an over-the-top, irrational and inappropriate way.

For instance, Tom was taking his turn cooking the family meal one night and was happily chatting away with his wife, Sarah, while she was folding up the clean washing. As he was opening a can of sweetcorn to add to his casserole, she happened to look up and exclaimed in concern, "Oh, you're not opening another big can of sweetcorn, are you? There's already a bowl of leftovers from the can we opened the other day in the fridge!" At this Tom flung down the wooden spoon he'd been holding and roared at Sarah, "You want to be in charge? *You* do the cooking, then!" Then he stormed out of the kitchen, slamming the door violently, and strode out of the house. Sarah, unsurprisingly, was shocked and upset.

On another occasion, Tom, Sarah and their two children were playing a board game. Tom thought he remembered the rules but the children, who had read the instructions on the box, said his version was wrong and they wanted to play it the right way. But Tom, insisting that his way was the original way to play, threw back his chair so that it smacked down loudly on to the floor and told them in no uncertain terms what he thought of *their* version of the game, before marching out of the room.

On both occasions, and others like it, Tom berated himself for his reactions later. But he had felt powerless to act differently at the time.

Joe has long been fascinated by what might drive such seemingly illogical behaviour, and several years ago set about researching the possible causes. After a lot of thought, he has developed a new theory that both explains much of this sort of irrational, undesirable behaviour and shows how, once identified, it can be dealt with remarkably simply. The method has since been used successfully countless times, not only by Joe but also by other therapists who work from the human givens approach.

Pleasure versus pain

At its basis is the understanding that a great many desirable experiences come at a price. To be able to survive, all animals must be able to weigh up whether pursuing instincts such as the urge to eat, drink, mate or sleep will be safe at the particular time they desire to do them. A meat-eating animal is hardly likely to decide to tuck into the tasty carcass of a kill if another animal higher up the food chain is lurking nearby, ready to pounce on it in turn. But often risks do have to be taken – winning a desired mate may require fighting off a rival; hunting sizeable prey may bring injury to the predator, as the prey fights back, etc. So, Joe reasoned, since animals must have evolved a method – which we, in turn, have inherited – for weighing up risks and benefits (the likely degree of pain or pleasure) on the basis of past experience, we must store any pleasurable element and any painful element of a past experience as *separate* emotional memories.

This means that, when a particular action brings both intense pleasure *and* intense pain, the memory of it is coded in such a way that, if similar circumstances arise again, we will pattern match unconsciously to the original situation but, in order to assess risk, the pain associated with that occasion will be brought to mind first. If there is a high risk of experiencing pain again in the new situation, we are unlikely to repeat the action and won't even be aware that there was ever a pleasure element the first time around. However, if circumstances dictate that, this time, we won't experience pain or we can take action to avoid it, then the pleasure associated with the original situation can surface and we act on the urge to experience it.

It is important to stress, however, that we are not talking about a *rational* process, where we carefully weigh up the pros and cons before acting (we would have become a predator's dinner by the time we'd finished doing that!). We are talking about *instinctive* reactions, designed to keep us safe, which happen very quickly and without conscious thought.

This instinctive process protects us from rushing blindly for a reward and ignoring the associated dangers because, if the dangers are too serious for us to risk, we remain completely unaware of the possible pleasure to be had from the situation.

Molar memories

Although it might not seem obvious at first, the pleasure aspect of such memories can be derived from anger, because it is a strong emotion, which can often be satisfying to express. So anger, too, will be suppressed if there is also overriding pain associated with the memory of a particular action or event.

Joe has given the name *molar memories** to painful or traumatic memories that have roots both in pleasure (including anger) and pain. This is because we usually think of a molar (grinding) tooth as having two roots (though in reality, it can have more) and a 'molar memory' also has two roots: pain and pleasure.

And, just as a molar tooth's roots have to be exposed or drilled by a dentist, if they become infected and need treatment, so the problematic emotional memory with its two roots has to be exposed and treated. Then it ceases to cause problems. We will illustrate exactly what we mean by this in a moment by continuing with Tom's story, as it provides us with a perfect example of anger as the hidden pleasure.

As in Tom's experience, most people have no idea of the cause of their irrational, inappropriate anger. They only know that it keeps occurring, however often they determine to act differently. When testing to see if a molar memory is the cause of someone's anger outbursts, Joe will encourage the person to re-experience the irrational anger by first recalling a recent incident that induced it. He then asks them to stay with the

---

* For more information about Joe Griffin's molar memory conditioning theory, see Griffin, J and Tyrrell, I, Eds, (2007) *An Idea in Practice: Using the human givens approach*, HG Publishing, East Sussex.

angry feeling but not to act on it (by just sitting there quietly, perhaps with their eyes closed, being aware of the angry feeling). He has found that, when people do this, some significant event from their past, most commonly from childhood, will usually float into their mind. (Most of the situations in which we experience a conflict between intense pleasure and pain tend to occur for the first time when we are young and are also quite likely to have been traumatic.)

However, if the problem is caused by a molar memory, the feeling they will initially recall when remembering the event came to mind will not be the feeling of anger they have now. It will be a painful one, and almost invariably a memory of feeling deep humiliation – perhaps due to being cruelly told off by their parents in front of other people, being laughed at by other children or being made a fool of by a teacher. However, if they stay focused on their current anger feeling, the anger will eventually manifest itself as an emotion they also experienced at the time, but didn't express.

The vegetable plot

As he was becoming extremely concerned about the effect his explosive anger was having on his family, Tom decided to visit Joe for help. Having discussed what was troubling him, Joe asked Tom to get back in touch with the feeling of anger that took him over when he yelled at Sarah and his children. Tom had no difficulty whatsoever in doing so. Joe then asked him to stay with that feeling of anger and see what, if anything, came into his mind. After a short while, what came up for Tom was a distinct memory of, as a child, planting potatoes for his father in the vegetable plot in their garden. Other children were helping, as were his younger brother and sister, and he was proudly showing them what to do. Then his father stormed out of the house towards them and, in front of them all, roared, "No! No! No! You are doing it all wrong, you stupid, stupid boy. Now I'll have to dig everything up and do it again myself!"

Tom recalled how humiliated and ashamed he had felt as he stood there. One minute all the kids had been looking up to him; the next, he was a laughing stock. He was frozen to the spot, unable to move, as his father continued to bawl him out and then grabbed the very spade Tom had been using to dig, making Tom feel even more useless and powerless. Joe told Tom to stay both with the memory and with the feeling of anger that had led that memory to come to mind. After a short while, Tom realised that, as a small boy out there in the vegetable plot, facing his irate father, he had also felt intense rage but, as a child, of course, he had not been in a position to express it. Indeed, he had been frozen in shock.

> 66 As a result, whenever he felt he was being criticised in any way, he would pattern match to that earlier experience. 99

Joe encouraged Tom to say now what he wished he could have been able to say then to his father. After a moment, Tom said urgently, with strong feeling, "How *could* you humiliate me like this, dad? I was trying to help! I was doing my best! I didn't *mean* to do any harm! You shouldn't treat me like this! You should treat me and my feelings with respect!"

> 66 When excessive anger is driven by a molar memory, the person is always blind to the source of it. 99

In terms of Joe's theory, it seemed that Tom had experienced both highly painful humiliation as a result of being criticised so publicly and, simultaneously, anger, which he had suppressed. As a result, afterwards, whenever he felt he was being criticised in any way whatsoever, he would pattern match, unconsciously, to that experience. If the risk of pain (humiliation) seemed strong – for instance, while still a child and still fearful of the power of his parents and teachers to humiliate him further – his anger stayed suppressed. But, once he was a tall, strong adult, it became safe for him to vent his anger against critics who were physically less powerful than him (his wife and children) – though, of course, it only made him feel good immediately afterwards, not later.

So, to recap, an individual whose excessive anger is driven by a molar memory is always blind to the source of it, because the positive feeling of anger will be screened from consciousness by the negative feelings associated with instinctive 'risk assessment'. If the risk assessment concludes that it is too dangerous for him or her to express the anger, then the feeling of anger won't enter their conscious awareness at all. On the other hand, if the risk assessment concludes that it is safe to express the associated anger (in Tom's case, because he was physically more powerful than his wife or his children), then that reaction is reinforced for the future *without* the person ever being aware of where the original motivation came from. Indeed, not knowing otherwise, Tom would have remained convinced that his anger was always aroused by some understandable cause, such as Sarah's comment about the sweetcorn or his children's refusal to play the 'right' version of the game. Continuing in this vein would have condemned him to repeat his anger outbursts in such circumstances again and again, reinforcing the excessive reaction still further and making it even easier to trigger anger outbursts in the future.

> 66 Tom shook his head in amazement. 'I feel no anger or arousal, at all.' 99

However, after Tom had finally expressed the anger he had felt towards his father that day in the garden, Joe asked him to think again about the various incidents with Sarah and the children, and asked whether he still felt anger. Tom shook his head in amazement. "I feel no anger or arousal, at all," he said.

Tom came back for another session with Joe two weeks later and was delighted to report that, although there had been several occasions on which someone had made a remark that he would previously have interpreted as criticism and become explosively angry about, he had been perfectly able to stay calm each time and even consider the value of whatever comment had been made. Because, in the first therapy session, he had, in effect, expressed his anger towards whom it was directed (his dad) at the time it was experienced (the garden incident), his brain could now identify that anger as belonging to the past, with no further relevance in future situations involving critical comments. Getting him to express it in the way he would have *liked* to at the time put it back in its proper context, so that it ceased to come up at inappropriate times anymore.

This is an enormously powerful way to undo the damaging conditioning that can be the cause of the irrational, 'over-the-top' anger outbursts that blight many lives.

Why men and women drive each other wild

Imagine this scenario: Rob comes home from work one evening to be greeted by his very flustered wife, Helen.

"I've had such a bad day!" she says to him. "I couldn't take Amy to nursery because she had a temperature and she's been completely out of sorts all day. So I had to cancel my dentist appointment, which took me weeks to get on a day I could go. Then Jack's school rang to say that he'd been tripped over in the playground by one of the other children and had hit his head. Jack was fine, they said, but, when that happens, they have to phone the family. I didn't know whether I should go and get him anyway, and take him to casualty for a head X-ray, but the welfare assistant was adamant he was okay. Still, I was worrying all day till he came home. He said that boy Brian down the road deliberately tripped him. I don't know if he did or not but I'm thinking about talking to his mother. Although maybe that will make it worse? I don't know. Jack doesn't want me to, of course, but is that because he's scared of being bullied?

"And, just when I was talking to Jack about that, Adrian's school rang to say that he's behind with his maths homework again. He keeps telling me he hasn't got any but the maths teacher says he's missed two lots now. I think Adrian just doesn't listen properly and so doesn't write it down. I know we agreed that, if he missed any homework again, he would not be allowed to play in the next school football match but, the thing is, he's been a sub up till now and in this next match he's been asked to play the whole game which would do *so* much for his confidence – but we did say he wouldn't be able to if he didn't do his homework, so I'm not sure –"

At this point, Rob breaks in and says, "It's all quite straightforward, Helen. You've got to let Jack sort it out with Brian for himself, if there's anything to sort out. It's not healthy to keep jumping in all the time – and I'm not surprised he doesn't want you to. And, if we said Adrian couldn't play the next game if he didn't do his homework, then he misses the game."

And, pleased with himself for sorting all that out in record time, Rob settles down on the sofa in the living room with the paper. Meanwhile, Helen is absolutely seething with anger. She bangs around in the kitchen for a while, then comes into the room and angrily declares, "You can serve up your own dinner, and keep an eye on Amy, as well. I'm going out!"

She storms out of the house leaving Rob completely nonplussed and now rather angry himself.

We all know that men and women think and handle emotions very differently from each other. Women tend to trust their emotions, men don't. When men talk, they tend to talk about facts and 'things' – cars, sport, politics, work, and

Why we get more angry with those we love

IT IS a sad fact of life that we very often express anger towards those we least want to hurt. Here are some of the reasons that those we are closest to get the worst of us as well as the best.

Proximity Because we spend a lot of time in close contact with those we live with, the chances are much higher of things happening that annoy or frustrate us. The irritating things that loved ones do tend also to be cumulative. We are much more prepared to overlook the annoying traits of an overnight guest – "Dear old Lisa. She never thinks to help clear up after dinner – just sinks into an armchair, like she's the lady of the manor." But when it is a son, daughter or partner who, day after day, doesn't help wash up or leaves the towels on the floor or never turns lights off – or moans about mess – it really winds us up.

Emotional investment As we have an emotional investment in our partners and children, we are strongly motivated to encourage them to make the best of themselves – and that means changing their ways, if we don't approve of them! Our expectations of them are, therefore, high but may differ, of course, from their expectations of themselves. A wife may be ambitious for her husband or children, while they perhaps are more interested in doing a job they enjoy, which isn't overly stressful. Parents want their children to work hard at school and do their homework, while children may think having fun is much more important. This sort of thing can lead to lots of nagging and friction.

Commitment We feel more confident about expressing our true feelings to those we love – and that includes anger – if we are ▶

so on – and they like to show what they know, such as how something works, as this satisfies their need for status. When women talk, however, they hope to glean information and to build rapport and understanding. They talk about people much more than they talk about things and, in general, they are more interested in emotions than facts. They will often get some of their need for status met through their social roles, or from knowing the latest bit of news. Men tend to be more goal-oriented and like to solve problems; women are more relationship-oriented and like to convey and discuss feelings. Men like to compete; women like to cooperate.

This makes for an interesting world but, alas, a lot of difficulties in relationships, if couples don't realise just how

in it for the long haul. If couples share a home, have a shared mortgage or split the rent, share a car and/or have children that they are bringing up together, these are signs of long-term commitment, and that makes both partners feel more secure about taking risks, such as losing their tempers over big or little things. As a result, we may well find ourselves speaking to our partners in ways that we would never dream of speaking to friends, because the friends would fairly quickly choose not to be around us.

None of this is to say that criticising or letting off steam at our loved ones is okay. But it helps to know why our thresholds for anger might be lower with those we love because, once we have understanding, we can do more to bring about change.

differently men and women behave and think. Helen, for instance, simply wanted sympathy for her anxieties and the chance to talk through her conflicting feelings. Her need was to be listened to. But Rob perceived a 'problem' and his need was to solve it, which he did.

So often women think their partners are heartless brutes if they refuse to discuss some relationship concern or walk away from an argument about it. But, in fact, men just aren't up to heated emotional discussion. During an argument, men's blood pressure and heart rate rise significantly higher that that of women and stay higher for longer. So, when men instinctively walk away, it is to stop their blood pressure soaring sky high and putting them at imminent risk of a heart attack. (They probably don't realise that is the reason for walking away, of course; they just know that they cannot cope with their uncomfortably heated feelings.)

> 66 Helen simply wanted sympathy and the chance to talk through her conflicting feelings. 99

Unfortunately, while walking away may help men to cool down (and, as they are better able than women to compartmentalise feelings, they can quite easily go off and do some gardening or tinker with the car and put the argument completely out of mind), women are left all wound up with their emotional arousal, deprived of the chance to express it fully and get their partner to 'see' why they are so distressed.

This may seem like a no-win situation – either the man or the woman is going to suffer, and that will no doubt lead to the other paying the price eventually as well. But it need not be so. If couples develop a better

> 66 When men walk away, it is an instinctive way of stopping their blood pressure from soaring sky high. 99

understanding of each other's emotional needs, most serious arguments can be avoided altogether. We explain the art of couple communication in the next section.

Ready to do something different?

By this point, you should have gained some new understandings about the nature of anger, which may have given you completely different expectations about handling it effectively, to the huge benefit of yourself and others.

In the next part of this book, we show you many important ways in which you can change your behaviour, so that you, or other people in your life, don't get so angry in future. Because the human givens approach works in line with human nature, everything you read in the following pages is readily achievable. All you need is a sincere desire to do so.

PART 2

Overcoming anger

*F*OR MORE than 20 years, we have worked successfully with countless adults whose relationships, work lives and social lives were being blighted by their out-of-control anger. We have also worked with a great many children who couldn't control their anger until they were helped to understand and handle it. These were people who needed the extra help that effective therapists can give – perhaps because their anger originated in traumatic experiences, like those we have just looked at. But we also know that it has been possible for many others to turn their lives around without professional help (in the same way that most ex-smokers gave up without help), just by using the powerful methods that we are going to share with you in this section.

As is the case with any strong emotion, when we are angry our higher intelligence disappears (even if the feelings of certainty that the anger generates fool us into believing other- wise). As we discovered in Part 1, anger makes us stupid! The more aroused we are, the less clearly we can think and the less chance we have of preventing a potentially manageable conflict situation from escalating out of control. So the ability to calm down, especially at vital moments, is an absolutely key weapon in tackling the tendency to be quick to anger and high arousal. Only by preventing our emotional brain from taking over can we keep our sense of perspective. We then have a better chance of seeing others' point of view and of coming to more rational conclusions instead of black-and-white ones.

> 66 ... you also need to stop your body feeling constantly tense and on the alert ... 99

So, if you suffer from inappropriate anger outbursts, your number one priority must be to learn a quick and reliable way to calm down, a method which you can use anywhere at any time so as to reclaim your intelligence and protect yourself from saying and doing stupid things. If you suffer from chronic anger, you also need to stop your body from feeling constantly tense and on the alert, as this causes stress hormones to keep on circulating. The best way to do both is to learn an effective relaxation technique.

Learn how to relax

Showing people how to calm themselves down is usually an important part of a first human givens therapy session. And most people find this an enormously helpful – and enjoyable – experience. For those who are chronically angry, and have lots of hostile thoughts running through their minds ("Who does he think he is? "How *dare* she ignore me?" "I was first in the queue, not him!" "Young people these days …", "You've got another think coming if you think I'm going to do such and such!"), it is like getting permission to stop being on constant alert for any perceived slights from others. After all, that is what most anger is about – a perception of unjust treatment. When you relax, you can concentrate on yourself for yourself, not in relation to anyone else, and simply appreciate being in your own body.

Another reason that learning to relax is so important is that we all endure many situations in a day that we cannot control and which raise our stress levels. If we are stuck in traffic, or on an unmoving train, or waiting for a bus for what seems like an interminable age, it is easy to get irritable and wound up. This is on top of the other demands of daily life, such as juggling work and child-care, working with a difficult colleague, caring for a difficult sick relative at home or struggling to deal with debt. The more stressed we become by such events, the more likely we are to explode over something trivial.

Yet, if you spend a lot of time feeling wound up and tense and always on the edge of an angry outburst, you may well feel doubtful that you could ever relax again! But, in all our years of experience, we have never come across anyone who couldn't be helped to relax for at least a little while, even those who were utterly convinced that it couldn't be done, or were actively resistant. However, we don't force people to relax 'our way'.

> 66 ... it will show you that things *can* be different. 99

What is important is to find the way that works for you. And there *will* be a way. For your body will be yearning for relief from the highly unnatural state of unrelenting stress you may unwittingly be subjecting yourself to. A short period of calm, whether 10, 15 or 30 minutes, is a wonderful gift to give yourself. It will show you, through the very experience of different sensations in your own body, that things *can* be different; you *can* make changes happen.

Once you know what true relaxation feels like (and many people tell us that they had quite forgotten), you will soon become able to relax yourself quickly whenever you need to. That means that you will have the ability to turn down the heat (in other words, lower your emotional arousal) on the spot, wherever you are – and without having to do anything that anyone else can see you doing, or needing to go anywhere special to do it. This is such a simple, effective first step for preventing anger from escalating into disaster. By leaving you access to the full power of your thinking brain, it lets you see the bigger picture instead of losing your cool.

A few ways to relax quickly

Here are a few easy and effective methods you can use to induce relaxation – choose one you like or try them all out, and then practise the one you like best for 10 minutes at least twice a day. If you find you are unable to relax by yourself at the beginning, doing some non-aggressive aerobic exercise (such as brisk walking, running, cycling or dancing) before the relaxation exercise could well help, as this improves mood, has a calming down effect and will create the spare capacity in you to relax more deeply. Or you could see a therapist so that they can do a guided relaxation process with you. We often record such sessions, so that our clients can replay them and induce a relaxed state whenever they want to. Alternatively, you might like to ask someone to read to you, for the first few times, the steps set out below, so that you can focus all your attention on relaxing.

> **66** This is such a simple, yet effective first step for preventing anger from escalating into disaster. **99**

1. The 7/11 method

Many people find that the easiest way to relax is to concentrate on their own breathing, so we suggest you try this method first.

- Settle yourself comfortably in a place where you won't be disturbed. Make sure your clothes are loose.

- Sit or lie comfortably with your hands side by side in your lap, or your arms by your side, and your legs uncrossed.

- Close your eyes.

- Now concentrate on becoming aware of your feet on the floor, your legs and arms where they are resting and your head against the cushion, pillow or chair back.

- Keep your shoulders down and take in as deep a breath as you can manage. The air is pulled down to the bottom of your lungs when you breathe in deeply and this makes your stomach inflate, like a balloon. So, to make sure you are breathing deeply, it can help if you put your hand on your stomach, and feel it swelling.

- Now breathe out – you will feel your stomach deflate again – and make each out-breath last longer than your in-breath. (This is important because the out-breath stimulates the body's natural relaxation response. By changing your pattern of breathing in this way, your body automatically begins to relax.) A good way to ensure that you are doing this is to breathe in slowly to the count of 7, then breathe out more slowly to the count of 11. If you cannot breathe out for that long, hold your breath for the remainder of the time while you keep counting to 11 and then breathe in again. Alternatively, try breathing in to the count of 3 and then out, more slowly, to the count of 5.

- Also make sure you breathe in and out through your nose and keep your mouth closed. This warms and filters the air that you inhale and prevents you from losing too much carbon dioxide when you exhale. (Carbon dioxide is needed to help the cells of the body use the oxygen that you are breathing in.)

- Do this slow breathing between 10 and 20 times, knowing that you will relax even more with each out-breath.

- Concentrate on the counting. Try not to let your mind wander off but, if it does, just gently bring your attention back to the counting.

- Try and be aware of how much less tense you feel, just by relaxing your breathing and blocking out over-busy thoughts.

- Most importantly – persevere! Most people who are stressed breathe too shallowly. They take quick, short breaths that take air down no further than the top of the lungs. If your shoulders rise as you breathe in and fall as you breathe out, you are taking shallow breaths. And, if that is the case, breathing in the new way we are describing may feel odd to you at first. Some people even say, "But it doesn't feel like real breathing!" Be assured, it *is* real breathing and far better for you than quick, panicky breathing. So it really is worth persevering. A great many people find that learning relaxed breathing completely changes their lives for the better, because it starts to put them in charge of their emotions.

This 7/11 (or 3/5) technique is good for instant calming down too. Just do it a few times, wherever you are, if you feel yourself getting wound up. No one will know that you are doing it, so there is no need for embarrassment.

2. The clenched fist method

Another good way to relax is through the following simple method, derived from yoga. (However, only use this if you don't have any problems with your hands, such as arthritis.)

- Settle yourself comfortably and then make your hands into the tightest fists possible. (If this is painful because your fingernails are long, just clasp both hands tightly together, interlocking the fingers.)

- Look at your fists carefully as you scrunch them harder and harder, being aware of the whiteness of your knuckles, the feeling of your nails against your palms, the pressure of your thumbs against your forefingers and the rigidity of your wrists. Notice, too, the tension moving up your arms to your elbows and shoulders.

- Keep squeezing your fists like this and concentrate on the physical sensations for a moment or two. To help you do this, close your eyes.

- Then, with all your attention focused on how that tension feels, allow your fingers and hands to slowly unwind, and concentrate on the changing sensation of growing relaxation.

- Still with your eyes closed, feel the enjoyable sensation of relaxation spreading quite naturally through your fingers and up along your arms as the tension drains away. You may find it takes the form of whatever your body needs – coolness if you tend to be too hot or warmth if you tend to feel too cold – or else you might just feel a pleasant tingling sensation.

- Whatever form it takes, let the relaxing sensation spread through your body, relaxing your brow, your cheek muscles, your jaw, your shoulders, chest and so on, down to your toes.

- Keep your focus on the stress falling away and the calming differences you can sense in your body, perhaps imagining the stress draining away from your body through the tips of your toes and disappearing into the ether.

- You can repeat this for as long as you like, while you enjoy noticing the calming changes that occur through-out your body. As your body relaxes, so does your mind.

3. The whole body method

This highly effective method is also derived from yoga and achieves relaxation in a similar way.

- Work gradually through the main muscles of your body, tensing each in turn for a count of 10 and then relaxing them. As in the previous technique, this works on the simple mechanical principle that, if you tense muscles and then relax them, your muscles are always more relaxed afterwards than before you tensed them.

- Try starting with your feet, move up to your calf muscles, then your knees, your thighs, your tummy muscles and so on.*

---

* A helpful relaxation CD, *Relax: using your own innate resources to let go of pent-up stress and negative emotion*, is available from the publishers of this book. Call +44 (0)1323 811662 or order online at www.humangivens.com As well as relaxing you, using these techniques and others, the CD gives information about the benefits of relaxation.

Use your imagination fruitfully: create a 'safe and special place'

You can make relaxing an even more pleasant and rewarding experience by using the time with your eyes closed to waft yourself away in your mind to some pleasant imaginary place, or to a real place that you love to go to. People often choose to imagine walking on an empty beach by the sea, or in the mountains, or by a stream, or sitting peacefully in their own gardens. Children might choose their bedrooms, if they feel safe there, or creatively imagine themselves in a magical land or somewhere in outer space. The scene can be wherever you want it to be. If you are more relaxed when there are other people around, incorporate their presence into your imaginings too.

Perhaps you relax by doing something physical, such as playing football or squash, dancing, cycling or walking in the park, in which case visualise yourself enjoying that activity, if you prefer. Wherever you choose to be and whatever you choose to do there, concentrate on making the occasion as real as it can be. Really try to *see* the colours of the sandy beach, or the flowers or football shirts. *Hear* the sounds – the gentle whoosh of the waves, the rustling of leaves, the voices of the players. *Feel* the textures; *smell* the flowers. (You may well find that you are 'better' at visualisation than at hearing the sounds or smelling the smells, or better at the sounds or smells than visualisation: this really doesn't matter, as we all tend to have one sense that is more dominant than the others; just focus on whatever comes easiest to you.)

Our imagination is like a muscle; it thrives when it is being used, so give it a really good workout. Imagine your chosen scene in detail, so that you can truly make it your very own 'special, safe place', one you will always be able to call to mind and enjoy when relaxed – or to use to help you to relax, when you need to calm down very quickly.

If you do start to become aroused and full of angry feelings, deliberately try to calm yourself down in one of the ways we've just described. Just as it is impossible to contract and relax a muscle at the same time, so you can't be angry when you are in a relaxed state. And, as we have seen, when you are calm and free from pressing thoughts, even for a short period, you have access to the rational part of your brain and can more clearly recognise and question any black-and-white thinking.

> 66 If you misuse your imagination ... you are undermining your ability to think clearly. 99

Whatever dominates our imagination and thinking ultimately determines our lives, and our character. If you misuse your imagination by dwelling on the hurts that make you angry, the fears that make you anxious or the worries that bring on depression, you are undermining your ability to think clearly and develop into a fully rounded individual. In a relaxed state you can consciously use your imagination in constructive ways to solve problems and see the bigger picture – which is what imagination evolved to do – thereby dispelling the hurts, fears and worries.

Practise 'mindfulness'

Most of us don't spend enough time 'in the moment', absorbed in what we are doing: we are more likely to do things absentmindedly, while we think about what we have got to do next. People who suffer from chronic anger often spend a lot of time fretting about something that happened in the past, where they didn't get their way, and running scenarios through their mind in which they would have acted more forcefully. They may also have hostile fantasies about unwelcome events that haven't yet happened – for instance spending the weekend with a critical mother-in-law. Creating 'mindfulness', a technique for turning off thoughts, is a powerful antidote to all that, derived from Eastern meditative practices. Although it can seem hard to do at first, just because it is so contrary to our usual way of going about things, perseverance really does pay off. Try it for yourself, by following these simple steps:

- Choose to give your complete attention to a simple task you are familiar and comfortable with. For instance, if you are doing some decorating, be aware of all the movements you make, as you make them, one after another. Be aware of the paint brush or roller and the surface you are painting, its textures and colours. Let your focus be *entirely* on the activity you are engaged in and what you are seeing and sensing, but don't *think* about what you are doing.

- If a thought intrudes, whether it concerns what you are doing (for instance, "I'm getting tired", "I'm bored" or "I don't like this colour") or is about something else, just be aware that you are having the thought, then gently let it go and bring yourself back to the task in hand. Your aim is to experience what is happening right now, not to think or make judgements or have opinions.

- Whatever your chosen activity, whether it's cooking, eating, cleaning, DIY, gardening, brushing your teeth, changing a tyre, savouring a cup of coffee or anything else, follow the same pattern: be aware of every action you are taking, moment by moment, and the associated textures, colours, sounds and/or smells that you are conscious of as you go along.

Taking a little time to practise periods of 'mindfulness' like this will give you a welcome break from the niggles and worries that increase stress levels and make anger outbursts more likely.

Try to live more healthily

A good diet, regular exercise and getting enough sleep are important for keeping everyone healthy. However, there are particular benefits in terms of lowering emotional arousal and reducing aggression.

For instance, too much coffee can wire some people up. Certain food additives, such as particular preservatives and colourings used in some foods and sweets, can adversely affect susceptible children and cause agitated behaviour. There is also some evidence that eating highly processed foods, such as refined white bread, and dried fruits can cause aggression and hyperactivity in children.*

Forty per cent of the membranes of the cells in the brain are manufactured from fish oils, so omega-3 oils have an especially crucial role to play in healthy mental functioning. Indeed, there is now compelling evidence that inadequate levels of omega-3 fish oils are closely linked with emotional instability and aggression. Studies in America, England and Holland have all found that when violent young offenders were given a diet fortified with omega-3 for three months, their aggression reduced by an astonishing 37 per cent.

Alas, probably few of us eat enough fish to take in all the

---

* For more information on possible effect of foods on behaviour, contact the Hyperactive Children's Support Group: www.hacsg.org.uk

Be cautious with alcohol

THERE IS no harm in enjoying a few drinks occasionally. However, if you are prone to anger, be wary of overdoing it. As we saw earlier on page 15, emotional arousal itself makes the effects of alcohol more potent. So, if you are having a great time with friends in a party atmosphere, remember that this is exactly when you are most at risk of 'losing it', if an argument suddenly develops.

omega-3 that we need and the oil is particularly prone to damage during cooking. Unfortunately, too, fish is increasingly affected by pollution, so some people prefer to take a supplement instead.* There are many you can choose from, both in tablet or capsule form. It is advisable to buy the purest and most refined form possible. (We recommend *EyeQ*, available from Boots.)

Regular exercise is a great way of getting your body and mind back into equilibrium and also offers an immediate and safe way to discharge stress. Whether you feel wound up after a day's work or by an argument with your partner or boss,

---

* Although it is also a good idea for pregnant women to make sure that they get sufficient omega-3 fish oils because these are also essential for the healthy development of the baby's brain, it is best to eat fresh fatty fish or take purified omega-3 fish oil supplements (but not cod liver oil because this also contains Vitamin A which is harmful if taken in excess). However, because of the dangers of contaminants in sea water, pregnant women and those likely to conceive in the future are advised by the Food Standards Agency to eat no more than two portions of fish a week.

jogging across the park, playing a vigorous game of squash or tennis, beating a boxing bag or doing whatever other sporty activity you like, is an excellent way to get rid of irritation and anger without anyone else getting hurt!

If you can't get out to do some sort of sport, then some energetic scrubbing, vacuuming, digging in the garden – or even dancing to the radio – can have just the same positive effects.

When taking regular exercise, the crucial thing, of course, is not to run angry scenarios through your mind while you are doing it, about whatever went wrong during the day or whatever you currently feel aggrieved about. If that is difficult for you, it may be best to look for a form of exercise that you can do with someone else – a competitive sport, perhaps, where you have to concentrate on what your opponent or the opposing team will do next. However, if you really love having some time to yourself, and to walk, run or jog alone, try to stay 'in the moment' or to use the time to problem solve productively.

> 66 Whatever you choose to do – **make sure you enjoy it**! 99

Whatever you choose to do, **make sure you enjoy it** – otherwise you will view it as a chore to be avoided if at all possible.

Getting a good night's sleep is important because we need enough slow-wave sleep to restore our bodies and renew our energy, and we need dream (REM) sleep to discharge un-

Tips for a better night's sleep

1. It may sound obvious, *but go to bed earlier* if you go to bed very late and always wake up tired!

2. *Avoid drinking tea or coffee late in the evening.*

3. *Avoid drinking too much alcohol.* Having several drinks may indeed get you off to sleep but, in the middle of the night, once the alcohol has been metabolised, your body is in withdrawal and that wakes you up.

4. *Don't take exercise within two hours of bedtime.* But do exercise earlier in the day or evening.

5. *Have a milky drink or camomile tea before bedtime.*

6. *Have a relaxing warm bath or shower before going to bed.*

7. *Ensure you have a comfortable mattress*, not one that is old and saggy.

8. *Put up blackout curtains or blinds*, if necessary, to keep the light from waking you.

9. *Use the bedroom primarily for sleep.* Don't watch television in it or listen to loud, fast music, or do anything else that wires you up. Having sex is good, however – although sex stimulates, it discharges energy and so doesn't adversely affect sleep.

10. *Wear earplugs* if your partner snores, or noise disturbs you from outside.

11. *Make sure you're not too hot or too cold in bed.*

12. *Try spraying some lavender around the bed or use a lavender pillow.* Many people find the scent helps to induce sleep.

expressed emotional arousals from the day just gone, so that we can start the next day charged up and ready to go.

The views of experts differ as to exactly how much sleep we need. So we suggest this simple rule of thumb: if you wake up refreshed and energised and ready to start the day, you are getting enough sleep, however many hours you have had.

13. *Do not nap* at lunchtime or in mid-afternoon.

14. *Don't lie awake having anxious or angry thoughts.* Use one of the methods we described earlier for inducing relaxation and then take yourself off in your imagination to a peaceful, beautiful, quiet place. Give yourself the suggestion every so often that "sooner rather than later, I can drift off into a sound refreshing sleep".

15. *If you wake in the night, never reward the brain for remaining awake.* Some people decide, after lying awake for half an hour, to get up and watch a film or to have something to eat. But that, by 'rewarding' us, just encourages the brain to wake us up every night! Instead, if you are not asleep within 30 minutes, get up and do an *extremely boring task* that you really loathe doing. It might be working your way through a pile of ironing; doing your accounts; waxing the floor; sewing on buttons; or filling cracks in the walls in preparation for decorating. (Of course we realise some people enjoy such activities!) You could even invent a boring task, such as standing on one leg whilst reading the telephone directory out loud. As soon as you are really tired, however, abandon the task and go back to bed. Repeat if you are still awake 30 minutes later or wake again.

Do an 'emotional needs audit' on yourself

If you are familiar with any of our other books in this series, you will know that we place great emphasis on the emotional needs audit. This is because it is important to identify what is not going right in your life, so that you can take some practical steps to deal with it. As we have mentioned before, no one suffers from out-of-control emotions or mental illness if their needs are being met in balance and they are making the best use of their innate resources. Carrying out the audit should help you identify whether you are suffering excessive stress in one or more areas of your life as a result of important needs not being met, and help you see more clearly where you need to work towards changing your circumstances to reduce or eliminate it.

EXERCISE:

We would now like you to take some quiet time, when you are not likely to be disturbed, to think carefully about what is happening in your life at the moment.

If you have already identified yourself as a black-or-white thinker, you might be tempted to say that none of your needs is being met. But that is extremely unlikely to be true. Try to think hard about each of the following questions and be as honest as possible. Perhaps, as you consider them, you will find that many things are actually working well (or could be), but one big area of dissatisfaction is overshadowing the rest. Or maybe certain needs *are* getting met but not in the healthiest way for you (as when an adolescent's need to be connected to the community can be met by being part of an anti-social or criminal gang). If you are reading this book to try and understand the angry behaviour of your partner or child, or a close colleague or friend, try to put yourself in their shoes, as far as you can. The paragraphs below each question are intended as a guide, to get you thinking. As you read through them, try to think whether the manifestation of anger and aggression, in you or someone you care about, might be the result of particular unmet needs.

Do you feel secure?

For instance, do you live with someone with whom you have a loving and caring relationship, or is the atmosphere at home one of fear because of your partner's explosive or abusive behaviour? Do you feel fearful that your partner will stray or is your partner fearful that *you* might stray? (As we've mentioned, sometimes one partner is – whether knowingly or otherwise – verbally cruel and treats the other with disdain, in the hope that the person who feels put down will feel too bad about themselves to leave and find a more loving partner.) If you are a young person, is your parents' or carers' relationship a good one? And how about their relationship with you? Or do you feel you can never do anything right in their eyes and are constantly walking on eggshells, in case you incur their rage? Do they set you clear and fair boundaries, so that you know the 'rules' about what you can and can't do? Or are they too strict, making you want to kick out against their rules, or too lax, making you feel they don't really care what you do? If you work, is your work culture authoritarian or inclusive? Is your job secure? Are you confident at work, school or university, or do you feel undermined or bullied by your peers or boss? Do you dread social occasions where you don't know anyone? If you have a mortgage or rent to pay, can you pay it? Have you suffered a severe stress, such as being assaulted on the street or burgled at home and, if so, have you got over it? (If not, you could be suffering from post-traumatic stress, one of the signs of which can be outbursts of anger.)

> 66 Really think about each question – be as honest and probing as possible ... 99

Do you feel you receive enough attention?

And, if so, is it necessarily of the right type? For instance, do you spend most of your time doing things for other people, such as your children, partner or parents, at the expense of your own needs? Do you ever feel that certain other people sap your energy, wanting all your support and a sympathetic ear

How well are your emotional needs being met?

YOU MIGHT like to use this checklist when carrying out your own emotional needs audit. Rate, in your judgement, how well the following emotional needs are being met in your life now, on a scale of 1 to 7 (where 1 means not met at all, and 7 means being very well met).

- Do you feel secure in all major areas of your life?
- Do you feel you receive enough attention?
- Do you think you give other people enough attention?
- Do you feel in control of your life most of the time?
- Do you feel part of the wider community?
- Can you obtain privacy when you need to?
- Do you have at least one close friend?
- Do you have an intimate relationship in your life (i.e. you are totally physically and emotionally accepted for who you are by at least one person)?
- Do you feel an emotional connection to others?
- Do you have a status in life (whatever it may be) that you value and that is acknowledged?
- Are you achieving things in your life that you are proud of?
- Do you feel competent in at least one major area of your life?
- Are you mentally and/or physically stretched in ways which give you a sense of meaning and purpose?

If you have scored any need at 3 or less, this is likely to be a major stressor for you.

Even if you have scored only one need very low, it can be enough of a problem to have a serious, adverse effect on your life, and could well be the cause of your anxiety/stress.

at any time that suits them, but are prepared to give little back? Are there people who are genuinely interested in what you think and feel? Do you feel appreciated? Do you spend more time alone than you really want to? Do you feel too shy to participate much on social occasions or fear them so much that you avoid them altogether? Do you get attention by 'kicking off', or by creating scenes and dramas? Or do you enjoy being the centre of attention through, for instance, giving speeches or seminars or presentations or performing on stage?

Do you think you give other people enough attention?

Do you enjoy spending time doing things with (or for) other people, such as your friends, children, relatives or needy neighbours – or do you resent what you perceive as demands on you? Do you 'hear' what your partner says to you and try to understand what he or she is feeling, or do you hear only what you expect to hear? Do you listen to what colleagues have to say or do you get irritated with them? Do you engage in certain activities just to win attention – turning to politics, for example, or taking up a sport, just to share the interests of the new love in your life or impress your boss? Are you genuinely interested in what others think and do, or just in how their opinions and actions affect you? If you have children who have outbursts of anger or temper tantrums, do you give them attention for their bad behaviour (by making a fuss about it, or telling them off) but not enough for their good behaviour (by failing to comment or praise them when they do something right or something kind)? Or are you just too busy to give them much attention of any type at all?

Do you feel in control of your life most of the time?

For instance, do you have sufficient responsibility in your work life, too little or perhaps too much? Do you have targets or deadlines that you struggle to meet? Can you take the responsibility for important decisions in your life or does someone else (a boss, dominating partner or parent) always make them for you? Does someone in your life have too much influence or power over you? Or do you have too much power over someone else (a child, a partner, a demanding relative) and deprive *them* of a sense of control? Have you, perhaps because of the arrival of a new person at work, a new baby or the introduction into your life of difficult in-laws, recently lost some of your sense of control? Do you feel you should be able to control things that, in fact, you can't – such as how much your children study or how well they do in exams – and blame yourself if things don't turn out as you think they should? Have you developed a physical disability or chronic illness that has taken away a measure of your control? Do you

> 66 Have you recently lost some of your sense of control? 99

have debts and other financial worries that you feel you cannot control? Do you feel out of control of your body or your thoughts (resulting in aggression or angry outbursts?)

Do you feel part of the wider community?

Humans are social animals and need social connections. Do you know people outside your close family and circle of friends? Do you help others, such as neighbours, or do voluntary work of any kind? Are you involved with a church or other religious institution? Or any neighbourhood schemes or local politics? Do you participate in any community activities, such as a local drama group, football team, aerobics class or parents' group? Are you, perhaps, a school governor or a member of a charity's management committee? Do you have people you say hello to on the street? Have you ceased to participate in regular activities because of a particular changed circumstance, such as the loss of a job, a newborn baby or a disability or chronic illness? If yes, do you feel resentful about that?

Can you obtain privacy when you need to?

Do you have anywhere in your home that you can withdraw to, where you can quietly reflect or get on with some task or hobby in peace? Do you have a space that is deemed yours, whether a bedroom or a study or a tree house or a den? Do you feel at screaming point because your 'space' is constantly being invaded by family members – or do you welcome being at the hub of family life? Do you work in an open plan office and, if so, does it offer any measure of privacy, such as screen partitions? Do you feel that your private belongings are respected, and not pried into? Can you/do you take off somewhere

> 66 Do you feel your private belongings are respected, and not pried into? 99

alone, if you need to? Are you always available via mobile phone during the day and evening? Do you think of journeys, in the car or on public transport, as journeys from hell (mainly spent in traffic jams or on crowded trains or buses) or as times to be relished, because, wherever you are, you can be alone with your thoughts or a book?

Do you have at least one close friend?

Is there someone in your life you trust completely and who trusts you, and with whom you are in contact a lot? Do you see them often? Do you do things together? Do you see them less since you or they started a relationship with a new partner, or a new job? Do you care what they think about you? Do you want the best for them, and do they want the best for you? Could you call on them for help at any time? If you are lonely, do you drink to mask the feeling?

Do you have an intimate relationship in your life?

Do you feel totally physically and emotionally accepted for who you are by at least one person. (This could also be your close friend.) Is there at least one person who you know will always be in your corner, if the going gets tough? Can you tell them anything? Do they comfort or advise you, when you are down, and bolster your confidence, and enjoy your successes? Do they think you are fun or funny and a great person to be around? Can you be yourself with them? Or have you lost the person who meant most to you in your life? For instance, has a serious relationship recently ended? Or have your feelings towards your partner changed because of something they did that hurt you or made you lose your trust in them? Are you grieving for someone who has died? (Bereavement can make us feel sad and bereft for a long time but if you are still completely grief-stricken two years after a loved one's death, that is no longer normal grieving.) Do you drink – or did you start – to mask the pain of bereavement or separation?

Do you feel an emotional connection to others?

Do you have family and friends you care about a lot, apart from your closest friend or your partner? Do you feel cared for by them? Do you speak to or see them often? Are rivalries and resentments common in your family, with someone or other not speaking to someone else a common state of affairs? Or have you lost touch with family or friends or stopped seeing them just lately? If you are the one with the angry or aggressive behaviour, has that led people you care about to not want to spend time with you or to ban you from their homes?

Do you have a 'status' in life that you value and that is acknowledged?

Do you feel that your relations, friends, partner, neighbours or colleagues respect you for the roles you play in life – for instance, as a parent or son or daughter, socially, at work, or as a talented musician, knowledgeable gardener, creative cake maker etc – and do you feel valued for how you carry out those roles? Do you

> **66** Do you feel suitably appreciated for what you do? **99**

feel suitably rewarded or appreciated for what you do? Are you admired or acknowledged by relevant people for at least one area of expertise? Do you feel you should have achieved more in life, or that others have done better than you and, if so, do you resent what you perceive as your failings and their success? Do you feel you fit in somewhere, or do you feel an outsider: a non-entity? Do you feel inferior or hostile to others or often jealous of them? Do you yearn for what you haven't got? Do you feel you have been denied chances in life?

Are you achieving things in your life that you are proud of?

We all need to feel a sense of achievement. On balance, are you doing what you want to do with your life or have you outgrown or lost interest in what you are doing now? Do you enjoy the way you spend your time and feel satisfyingly stretched by it or do you feel out of your depth? Do you like new challenges? Or do you avoid challenges and stick to what is comfortably familiar, blocking out the thought that perhaps you could achieve more? Do you feel unsatisfied, unchallenged or stuck, perhaps because there is nothing further you can achieve at work or your children have grown up and left home? Or are you resting on your laurels – relying on a major past success to feel good about yourself?

Do you feel competent in at least one major area in your life?

When we know we are competent at something, whatever it is, we have evidence that we are not useless. So, do you think you are good at at least some of what you do, whether that is being a parent, holding down a job, helping others, managing a career, playing a sport, or using an important life skill such as cooking, sewing, gardening, car maintenance or whatever? Can people rely on your skills? And do people respect them? If you don't feel competent, you are likely to have low self-esteem, which comes from a sense of inadequacy and lack of self-belief, and that can manifest itself in inappropriate anger.

Are you mentally and/or physically stretched in ways that give you a sense of meaning and purpose?

As we've seen, there are three main ways we find meaning and purpose in our lives. First, we all need to feel needed or that we can do something that is of value to others. Ask yourself, are there people in your life who need you? Do you have a caring role as a parent or adult child of elderly parents or within a caring profession? Do you engage in activities that have meaning for others, such as helping out in a charity shop, visiting elderly people, walking a sick person's dog? Second, we need to have activities that interest and continue to challenge us. (Even when we are retired from work, retirement from life is not an option: we need to stretch ourselves and set realistic goals to aim for, whatever our age.) Third, it helps enormously to have an overarching philosophy or commitment to something bigger than ourselves that makes life seem intrinsically meaningful. Consider whether you have such a commitment, be it spiritual, political, a determination to save the environment or to raise health standards in developing countries – something that holds wider significance for you than just your own concerns and gives your life direction and purpose.

What have you found out?

When you have completed your audit, you may well find that you have a lot of things going for you in your life and that it is unrealistic expectations or resentments that are actually causing the difficulties for you. Or you may have uncovered one or more clear areas of unmet need that could be triggering your anger or aggression or keeping it going. It could be that you have found that some of your needs are being met in unhealthy ways that are bad for your health or your relationships with others. If you have identified a traumatic period in your past, such as an abusive relationship you experienced as a child or an adult, or a seriously traumatic event of any kind, such as an assault, a car crash or a complicated childbirth, it may well be that you are still suffering, if unconsciously, from the emotional fall-out. You may need professional help to enable you to put the experience emotionally back into the past (see Part 3), to overcome your anger.

For those whose quick tendency towards anger is caused by an overload of stress, an extremely helpful piece of advice to keep in mind is the following.

Do what you can to change those circumstances that you can change. Stop giving time and thought to those that you can't control.

For instance, speak to your boss about being overloaded with work to the point that you can't perform any of your tasks satisfactorily. Look for some respite care for the sick relative you care for. Or get advice and help on how to handle debt.

If you are frustrated when being passed from one department to the next, when dealing with public services, or find your blood pressure rising when trying to sort out a complaint with a company (which keeps you on hold on the telephone and then offers unhelpful advice), remember you *can* take back control in such circumstances by making it your goal to stay calm. Although you can't control the outcome of your complaint, or whatever bureaucracy has been put in place, you *can* control your own responses. If you feel your concern is not receiving due attention, it is better to stay calm so that you can think straight enough to then ask, "How do I speak to someone more senior?", rather than lose your rag and screech in a demented fashion at a junior member of staff, who doesn't hold the power to meet your needs anyway.

> 66 You may well find that you have a lot of things going for you in your life ... 99

And, if your son or daughter is messing around instead of working for public exams, and you have done all you can to motivate them to work harder, don't waste your precious energy and time on extreme 'what if' scenarios, where you imagine them jobless and begging on the streets, and winding yourself up in frustration. (After all, some of the most successful people failed miserably at school.)

It is worth repeating – do what you can to change those circumstances you can change. But stop giving time and thought to, and getting agitated by, those that you *can't* control.

We hope you will now use whatever you have found out from the emotional needs audit to help you get the best out of the sections that follow.

Watch your self-talk

If you are someone who is chronically angry, you will have a lot of negative, angry, hostile and resentful thoughts churning around in your mind, even if you aren't aware of it most of the time. (If you have identified yourself as low in self-esteem, you probably have a lot of anxiety thoughts as well.) All this negative thinking takes up valuable energy reserves and serves to increase your stress levels – which in turn, lowers your threshold for tolerating annoyances – so it is of uttermost importance to stop this style of thinking as soon as you can. And one of the most effective ways to do this is by applying the ABC – **A**wareness, **B**lock, **C**hallenge.

Awareness – *Try to become conscious of your negative thoughts*

We all have a commentary that goes on in our heads; it is our own inner voice but hearing it is a bit like hearing a voice on the radio: we tune into and out of what's being said, depending on how strongly it catches our interest. However, not paying attention to a lot of what we think, continuing almost on automatic, doesn't mean that those thoughts aren't powerfully affecting us. They are! And as soon as we start to engage with angry or threatening thoughts, experiencing them as meaningful and real, the stress hormones will begin to circulate as we look to defend ourselves against imaginary danger!

Many clients, when we first ask them to become conscious of the content of their negative thoughts, choose to note them down in a notebook whenever they become aware of them. And they are usually shocked to find just how many come into their minds, over the course of a day. Here are some of the typical thoughts that come up for people whose anger is fuelled by hostile or anxious thinking. You may well recognise some:

"I never get given a chance."

"They just want to put me down."

"It's not fair!"

"How dare you!"

"I could have done that better than him/her."

"I can never do anything right in my boyfriend's eyes."

"I'm being taken advantage of."

"What a thoughtless/rude/stupid thing to do!"

"Why do I have to work with (sit next to/live with) morons?"

"I'm not giving way to *you*."

*"Just who **does** she think she is?"*

"I'm not good enough."

"I'll never be able to cope."

"I'm useless."

A lot of these thoughts might be the equivalent of knee-jerk reactions. You spill a bit of coffee or forget to post a letter and automatically you think, "I'm useless". Someone edges ahead in a queue or takes the last supermarket trolley, and again you automatically think, "It's just *not* fair!"

Other thoughts may be more specific to the circumstances. Perhaps a husband continues to read the paper while his wife recounts a sob story – fed up with no reaction, she gives up without him even noticing, and goes away, saying to herself, "He *never* listens to a single word I say, the *******!" Or a man is driving down a main road when a car pulls out of a side road ahead of him, causing him to slow down by the tiniest fraction. He thinks, "You did that *deliberately*, you *******!"

Only when you have become aware of your own negative

> **❝** ... within a short time, you will notice a huge reduction in negative thoughts. **❞**

thoughts will you be able to deal with them differently. So try to note down both types of thoughts, whenever they occur. Once you can easily spot them, you will then be able to choose to do either, or both, of the following and, within a short time, you will notice a huge reduction in such thoughts.

Block – *Refuse to go there!*

Try saying strongly to yourself, as soon as the thought has popped into your mind, "No! I'm *not* going to allow that angry (or anxious) thought to run through my brain!" Use your own words – ones that feel more natural to you. Some people simply say to themselves, "Stop!" or "No!" or "Go away, angry thought!"

Challenge – *Question the content of the thought*

Whenever you notice a negative thought, try examining it more closely, as if from an 'observer' standpoint. Very often, we just accept a thought's negative content without a moment's hesitation because we're on automatic and aren't paying it any attention. But now that you are no longer on automatic, you have the chance to assess whether you are being un-necessarily hard on yourself or other people. And the more you challenge automatic negative thinking, the less and less often such thoughts will pop up.

The following pages give examples of how you might challenge the negative thoughts we listed above.

"I never get given a chance."

"Actually, thinking about it, last week I was chosen to do such and such. So it isn't true that I *never* get given opportunities."

"They just want to put me down."

"I don't think they recognise all my skills. I'll have to find a way to show what I can really do."

"It's not fair!"

"You win some; you lose some. Life isn't fair for anyone."

*"How **dare** you!"*

"I feel insulted by that but I don't have to jump to conclusions."

"I could have done better than that!"

"They are clearly trying their best and that's what counts."

"I can never do anything right in my boyfriend's eyes."

"My boyfriend corrects me sometimes, if he thinks I'm not right."

"I'm being taken advantage of."

"I have no evidence for that."

"What a thoughtless/rude thing to do!"

"Maybe they didn't actually mean to be thoughtless/rude."

"Why do I have to work with (sit next to/live with) morons?"

"Nobody is a moron. I'm just feeling a bit cross with them at the moment."

"I'm not giving way to you."

"Actually, it won't be any skin off my nose if I let her go ahead. It will probably make me feel good."

*"Just who **does** she think she is?"*

"Poor woman. She probably doesn't realise how she is coming across."

"I'm not good enough."

"I'm doing my best and that is all anyone can do."

*"I'll **never** be able to cope."*

"I've always coped before. Why not now?"

"I'm useless."

"I've messed this up a bit but it isn't too difficult to put right."

Having stopped yourself from getting caught up in the angry (or anxious) thought in these ways – and it will only take a few seconds – now deliberately focus your mind on something else. Perhaps practise your 7/11 breathing or count backwards from 100. Or you could turn your thoughts to something nice that you are looking forward to or to some problem you need to solve or, if appropriate, go back to whatever you were thinking before the negative thought came into mind. Do anything positive that keeps you from engaging with the angry feeling.

Try taking a different perspective

Claire is upstairs getting ready for a night out with husband Tony, while he is waiting for her downstairs. Tony looks at his watch. "Look at the time!" he says to himself. "We should be in the restaurant by now! We should have been there *five* minutes ago! What will our friends think? This is so rude! What the hell is she doing? Twenty-five years of hanging around waiting – it's no joke! I should have left her waiting at the altar, that's what I should have done! Then where would she be? I can't believe any woman could take this long to get ready. It's not as if we are going to the opera! We're only going for a curry!"

This sort of self-talk is getting Tony nicely wound up, of course. He starts to pace, grows more and more agitated and, we can be pretty certain, will have more than a few harsh words for Claire when she does at last come down. She will retaliate in kind and the evening will be ruined.

But suppose Tony thinks like this instead: "Isn't it lovely that, after 25 years, Claire still cares enough to look nice when we are going out together. Martin and Julie won't mind if we're a little late – they've been late a few times themselves before now. I know, I'll use the time to take a quick look at the newspaper as I haven't had a chance yet ..."

Then, when Claire comes down, he will probably pay her a compliment, which she will appreciate, and they will leave in a good mood, ready to enjoy their evening.

What Tony has put into practice is one of the most powerful psychological techniques for changing behaviour. Therapists call it reframing. It means putting a different cast on an event and seeing the potential for a contrary interpretation of it. And, because you have to stand back and observe what is happening from a wider perspective, you can keep your cool instead of getting taken over by mounting anger – which, as we've seen, makes you temporarily stupid!

Reframing is a refinement of challenging negative thoughts. It lets you explore different options instead of rushing hotheadedly to adopt the one that is most damaging – for you or someone else.

EXERCISE: Widen your perspective

When you have a negative thought about someone else's behaviour or about something that has – or hasn't – happened, try coming up with a number of possible explanations for it, instead of sticking with the knee-jerk one you came up with first. As well as challenging your thoughts here, you are looking to reframe them in an entirely different light. For instance:

"He never cleans the bath after using it. He does it just to wind me up!"

"He probably doesn't even notice that the bath isn't clean because his mind is on other things."

"He hates cleaning; I hate gardening and leave it to him, so I suppose it works out fairly in the end."

"That woman driver cut in front of me deliberately!"

"She probably didn't see me. I know the parked cars make it difficult to see when coming out of that side road."

"My kids drive me mad! They won't do what I say!"

"They're just trying to get their own needs met. Sometimes our needs conflict and we have to find a way to compromise."

"That old woman at the head of the queue is counting every last little coin out of her purse to pay for that loaf of bread. She's doing it just to hold us all up!"

"That woman might be almost completely penniless till she gets her pension. I wonder if she had to raid the jar of coins she saves for her grandchildren, just to be able to afford bread to eat?"

"My child is stubborn."

"My child is clearly capable of standing up for herself and not getting bullied."

"How dare they keep me hanging on the phone, waiting to speak to someone, and expect me to pay for the call, when they made the mistake on my credit card bill!"

"The person who eventually answers my call is not the person who made the mistake. They are there to help but probably get shouted at all day, so I am going to be polite and respectful."

"My friend never bothers to arrive on time to meet me."

"Being late is just a feature of her easy-going nature, which is what I like so much about her."

When the joke's not funny

A policewoman once came to see Ivan because she kept becoming violently angry with her colleagues and even her boss. She knew her anger was associated with a horrible practical joke that had been played on her by her colleagues, using a dead body part. She had forgiven them for it but she still could not stop the anger taking hold. Her colleagues regretted what they had done and had expressed remorse for it, but they were now becoming fed up with her continuing irritability, tearfulness and anger, which just didn't abate. She wanted to stop reacting this way, as it was affecting her friendships and career.

Clearly, the shock of the 'joke' had traumatised her and the anger was a symptom. However, as well as detraumatising the terrible experience using the rewind technique (see page 197), Ivan also developed an extensive reframe about how this whole period in her life could be seen as a great learning experience. She had learned, for example, about thoughtless-ness – the unintentional harm people do to one another sometimes – and how in future she would be especially careful in how she behaved with others, as she knew only too well that sometimes a bit of 'harmless fun', or even a careless word, can damage people unintentionally.

After the session, the policewoman remarked how helpful she had found that shifting of her perspective.

Use these skills to become less self-centred

Using the ABC technique and the skill of reframing not only helps us lower our unhealthy emotional arousal; we also become less self-centred. When we get angry about perceived injustices or bad behaviour, it is because we think *we* are being personally targeted or personally slighted. We are constantly thinking that everything is about us. But most of the time, this just isn't true.

Suppose you are in the middle lane of the motorway, travelling at the correct speed and overtaking a lorry in the left lane, when a sports car suddenly swerves in front of you, illegally overtaking on the left because there is a car just ahead in the right-hand lane. You are forced to brake and nearly lose control of the car, while the kids are screaming in terror in the back. You manage to keep the car under control. Meanwhile, the sports car has swerved back into the right-hand lane just ahead, where it is clear. Seemingly, then, the crisis is over and disaster has been averted.

But the crisis *isn't* over because that alarming set of events has set the fight-or-flight reaction in motion. Blood is rushing to your muscles; your breathing is fast; your heart is thumping. You are in a highly aroused state.

What you do next will either save or cost you your life and that of your family. For, as your anger and emotional arousal soar, so your higher intelligence system shuts down. If you keep reliving what has just happened and cussing the sports car driver, even though he's long gone ("The idiot! He could have *killed* us all! He should be banned from driving! He's a lunatic!"), you may momentarily feel good but you risk shutting down your thinking powers altogether. And, paradoxically, although you are now in instinctive 'survival' fight-or-flight mode, losing access to your thinking skills may kill you all if, in the next few minutes, events require you to perform another instantaneous and skilled driving manoeuvre.

So, what should you do instead?

1. Do whatever is necessary to lower your arousal at once. Do a few rounds of 7/11 breathing; put on some calming music; count backwards from 100; and/or pull off the road to calm down further (see 'Take time out', below).

2. Come up with another way to view what has happened. For instance, "That person might be under some terrible pressure. Maybe his mother is dying or his wife is having

a baby and he has to get to the hospital fast." It doesn't matter whether you think this is likely to be true or not. Just creating another possibility in your mind will stop you from taking the event *personally* and that lets the emotional arousal start to drop.

3. If you can't be so charitable, even a thought such as, "He is the one who will suffer, if he carries on like that. Thank goodness he is nowhere near us anymore," will also serve to take away the sense of being on the receiving end of a deliberate or personal attack. The driver really didn't care who he was cutting up. He just wanted to get somewhere faster and took risks to do so, for whatever reason.

Take time out

This is an essential calming down skill to add, when needed, to those we've already discussed. And it means exactly what it says: if you are getting dangerously wound up, and you fear losing your cool completely, remove yourself from the situation for a while to give yourself time to calm down so that you can think straight again.

As we saw in Part 1, men's blood pressure and heart rate rise significantly higher than that of women when they get emotionally aroused, and it stays higher for longer. So it is very often essential that men, in particular, discontinue an argument, whether with a partner, colleague or annoying neighbour, before they lose all reason and do something they regret. But it's not only men; women also get highly aroused, upset and over-emotional about things that matter to them, and often benefit from a calming down time, too.

Don't just walk off, of course! Say why you are leaving, where you are going and for how long you expect to be gone. (Time out is about taking a break in order to calm down before resuming discussions, not about running away.) If you arguing with your partner, you could say something like, "This is a very important issue and I really do want to sort it out. But I'm starting to get too stressed to think straight, so I really need to take some time to calm down. Then we can continue discussing this more reasonably." Take at least 20 minutes, otherwise you will only have regained a superficial calm and at a physiological level you will still be aroused. As a result, if your partner then says something you find provocative, you are likely to hit the roof again in a matter of seconds.

Even if, when you ask for a break, your partner says, "But the babysitter will be here in 15 minutes!" or "I'll have gone out by then!", be firm and explain that it isn't possible to calm down properly in less than 20 minutes. If necessary, re-schedule the discussion for another day, making it clear that this is not a brush-off. Unresolved conflict is one of the main triggers for relationship breakdown. (If, however, you are about to go out together for the evening and you are arguing about something immediate, such as who is going to drive and who is going to be able to drink, then it is more appropriate to use the ABC and a reframe to give you the instant anger control that will let you both arrive at an acceptable solution.)

However, what you do in your 'time out' break is highly important! The aim is to calm down. If you spend it rehearsing all the justifications for your anger, you'll come back feeling even more angry, instead of calm. Choose, instead, to do something to dissipate the arousal. This could be 7/11 breathing, meditation or strenuous physical activity, such as jogging, housework or digging. You could even choose to sit and do the crossword in the daily newspaper, because that gets the thinking brain back centre stage, instead of the emotional brain. The trick is to do whatever works for *you*.

A different person!

Ruth and her husband Paul were having relationship difficulties caused, they both agreed, by Ruth's seemingly uncontrollable anger attacks. For both, it was their second marriage. Paul had a daughter, Emma, aged 15, while Ruth had a 19-year-old daughter, who was at university in the town where her father, Ruth's ex-husband, still lived. When Ruth arrived for therapy with Joe, both she and Paul were thinking they would have to end their relationship, if she couldn't get her temper under control.

It quickly became clear to Joe that the main trigger for Ruth's anger was Paul's emotional closeness with his daughter. She was jealous of the attention she saw Emma getting, especially as her own daughter wasn't around and had 'sided' with her dad, after the marriage break-up. Ruth, however, insisted that she was extremely familiar with teenage girl behaviour, having lived through it herself and with her daughter and her daughter's friends, and that her anger was caused by Emma's "completely abnormal" behaviour. Her anger took the form of critical outbursts against Emma or furious arguments about her with Paul.

Joe explained to Ruth that, when we get emotionally aroused, we cease to think straight and become convinced that we are right and that there is no other conceivable sensible view but our own. He then taught her the skills of ABC, reframing and 'time out', as a means of getting back perspective and being able to take a fresh look at an upsetting situation. By using those three skills, Ruth had her anger under control in just a few sessions. She was pleased to report back to Joe that, whenever she saw Paul and Emma being emotionally close and started to feel jealous, she would tell them she was going to her bedroom for a while to rest. Then she would lie on her bed and do 7/11 breathing. Once she was calm enough, she was able to take a different perspective. She would bring to mind recent memories of herself and Paul being close and how, in so many ways, he showed that he loved her too and wanted her as his life partner. When she did that, the jealousy subsided, and she was able to continue with a normal family evening.

> **The easiest way to change someone else's behaviour, is to change your own.**

In her last session with Joe, she said, in a bubbly voice, "You wouldn't believe how much my stepdaughter has changed! She's like a different person." And no doubt she was. For it's true that the easiest way to change someone else's behaviour is by changing your own. When Ruth stopped being critical and unpredictably angry, Emma could relax and relate to the warm side of Ruth.

Take back control of your imagination

One of the most misused of our precious innate resources is the imagination. Because the human brain is a problem-solving organ, what our imagination enables us to do, when used correctly, is to direct our attention away from our emotions so that we can solve our problems more effectively. If we are in a spot of trouble, for instance, it is far more productive to use our imagination to build on our past experiences and knowledge and come up with an inspired, intelligent solution to the current difficulty, than it is to use it to imagine emotionally arousing scenarios of the dreadful things that could happen if we don't sort the problem out.

Yet imagining such negative possibilities, or rerunning something annoying or frustrating that's already happened, is what so many people spend vast amounts of time doing. And that either keeps the anger building or generates the high level of anxiety that can result in sudden anger. The reason is this. The amygdala, the little organ in the brain that works as the security alarm, *doesn't know the difference between imaginings and reality.* It gets the body just as worked up and stressed if you are sitting comfortably at home imagining dunking your boss's head in a bowl of cold water as it would if you were doing it for real. Therefore, to take a different scenario, if you are driving down the road and another driver cuts across you, it is both futile and harmful to your own body to spend the next half hour seething and fuming and running preposterous violent fantasies through your head about what you would like to do to him if you could catch him.

Our imagination is such a powerful tool. Used positively, it can work as a reality simulator, letting us rehearse in our minds what it will be like to take actions for real. To give an example, suppose we are due to make a presentation to our colleagues. We have made all the necessary preparations but public speaking always makes us nervous. If, however, we take the time beforehand in a calm moment to envisage ourselves standing up confidently, walking to the front of the room, speaking warmly and firmly and at a suitable speed, perhaps cracking a joke to put ourselves and others at ease, and then working through our presentation in a way that will hold our audience's attention, we are far more likely to be able to produce that behaviour when the occasion comes. The brain always seeks to complete expectations that it has set for itself, and here the expectation is one of success. But if we spend the night before worrying that we will trip over, get our papers out of order, have to keep clearing our throats or that we'll lay into old Bruce if he comes up with one of his usual smart-arse questions, we are literally

> 66 The brain always seeks to complete expectations that it has set for itself ... 99

willing ourselves towards catastrophe!

So, if you are prone to anger, stop running scenarios and fantasies through your mind that make you start to rage and replace them instead with scenarios that put *you* back in positive control of your emotions. This is how Joe worked with Bill to do just that, and it literally changed Bill's life.

Heading for jail

Bill was 25 when he was referred to Joe by the court because of his severe problems with anger. One weekend, he had almost throttled his wife Angela to death in a rage of jealousy. The police were called and charges pressed but, then, because Bill genuinely loved Angela and she loved him and wanted him to have another chance, it was agreed that Bill should be allowed to give therapy a try instead, to help him get his murderous anger under control. He was told in no uncertain terms, however, that if there were one more episode like the last one he would be charged and sentenced.

Bill, as you can imagine, was highly motivated to sort out his anger problems. He told Joe that he and Angela had lots of great times together and really enjoyed each other's company but then he would get overwhelmed by the conviction that she was betraying him sexually and having affairs with other men. He admitted he had no shred of evidence for this belief. Bill had a very low sense of self-esteem, due to neglect in his childhood, and, as, deep down, he didn't rate himself as any great shakes, he couldn't see why any woman would want to be with him – especially someone as attractive and lively as Angela. Consequently, he was always anxious about losing her, although he hadn't been aware of that.

All he was conscious of was his belief that Angela made a fool of him in public because of the attention he thought she was giving to other men. When he was out with her and she was looking at him, chatting and laughing, he would suddenly become convinced that she was looking not at him but at someone behind him. If he turned around and there were two old ladies there, he would forget about the thought but, if there was a man there (even if he was with his *own* girlfriend and not paying Angela any attention), Bill would go into a silent rage and spend the rest of the evening watching to see where Angela was looking. He would then feed his fear by running pictures through his mind of Angela laughing, flirting and making love with whichever particular man had been sitting behind him – or had been next to them in the cinema queue, served them in a shop or wherever else it was that they were when Bill's insecurity and jealousy got the better of him. He was convinced that, if Angela left him, his life would be finished, so he frequently ran scenarios of despair through his mind as well, seeing himself as lonely and unloved.

Joe knew that the best way to help someone like Bill to

re-evaluate his self-worth was through guided imagery. In guided imagery, as its name implies, a therapist acts as a guide to help clients relax and imagine pleasant and positive scenarios for themselves. (You can also do this for yourself by following the instructions given in "Create a safe and special place" on page 93.) Then, while the client is deeply relaxed, the therapist

> 66 Although Bill hadn't been aware of it, deep down he was always anxious he would lose Angela. 99

encourages them to rehearse making the best use of their own innate abilities. (Again, you can do this for yourself, once deeply relaxed.) If we are relaxed when we envisage ourselves doing something differently, we are far more receptive to believing we can do it for real.

So first, Joe asked Bill to recount to him a few occasions when he and Angela had been totally happy in each other's company. Then he relaxed Bill deeply and reminded him, while relaxed, that all the evidence showed that Angela truly loved him. The very fact that she wanted to give him a second chance after he had almost murdered her showed her deep attachment to him.

Because of Bill's low self-esteem, it was important to say nothing that might be interpreted by Bill as a criticism of him, so Joe made sure that he sympathised with Bill's intentions, when he became angry, but not with the anger itself: "You want your relationship to last. It is deeply important to you. Unfortunately, the way you are going about it is threatening to destroy both you and Angela. It is the strategy that needs to change."

Joe then reiterated that there was no evidence of betrayal. But he also needed to build Bill's confidence in himself and his ability to attract and keep a partner, as he couldn't be sure of the eventual outcome between Bill and Angela (she might still decide to leave at some point). So Joe said to Bill, "Even if there *were* evidence of betrayal and it turns out that your partner is not worthy of the faith you have put in her, or if something else happens that leads to the end of the relationship, this is not the end of the world. If you succeeded in attracting one partner, you are more than capable of attracting another. You are handsome, intelligent and hard working. If you work hard at anger management skills, you have every chance of attracting a lovely person into your life. Why would you want a person in your life if they were going to betray you or make you unhappy? But Angela *does* love you and hasn't betrayed you. That is what the evidence shows."

Next, Joe guided Bill to run through his mind the memories of the numerous happy occasions he had spent with Angela. He then suggested to Bill that, at the times when he would usually have run his betrayal fantasies through his mind, he should bring to mind those happy memories and imaginings of future happy times, instead.

Finally, Joe encouraged Bill to spend some time visualising himself with Angela in a bar or restaurant, or a cinema queue, revelling in the fact that both were giving each other their full attention and were completely wrapped up in each other.

When Joe brought Bill out of deep relaxation, he also taught him 7/11 breathing, the ABC and the art of reframing. Bill was able to make good use of all these techniques. He turned his behaviour completely around. Now, many years later, he is still with Angela, has two children with her, and is no longer the victim of anger.

Psychic armour

You can also use your imagination in other ways to help you prevent anger arousal occurring in the first place, or to cool it quickly once aroused. For instance, a highly successful technique for helping yourself to stop flying off the handle, if someone makes a remark intended to annoy or hurt you, is to imagine that you own a suit of 'psychic armour', made of something like glass fibre or a magical gossamer-thin but immensely strong substance that you can slip over your head and entire body. You can breathe normally and move normally inside it and no one is aware of it but you. It is your psychic protection suit. When someone says something provocative to you that would normally make you see red, picture yourself in this suit and enjoy noticing the words bounce off it, without even getting close to you. You can hear the words and you can see the expression on the speaker's face but none of it connects with you. You just gleefully observe, from inside the suit, their surprise or disappointment when you don't respond as they expected. (It is a good idea, whilst nice and relaxed, to practise visualising yourself in such a situation, imagining seeing the insults bouncing off your protective suit and you continuing on your way unaffected.)

Glenys came to see Joe because she feared her behaviour was putting her job at risk. Her immediate boss was rather a bully. He would regularly criticise her work and she would frequently react by getting angry and answering back. This could lead to quite a slanging match, so much so that on one occasion it resulted in their both being hauled up before senior management and getting reprimanded. Glenys was desperate to learn how to control her feelings. Joe did guided imagery with her, relaxing her deeply and guiding her through a walk in her special place (she had chosen a walk along the beach on a bright, windy day). As she sat, calm and relaxed, with her eyes closed, enjoying the imagined scenery, Joe introduced to her the idea of psychic armour:

"I'd like you to imagine you have in your possession an almost invisible glass fibre suit that you can slip over your head and body. It is invisible to everyone else and it is your protection. If, in future, someone says something provocative that would make you respond angrily, it will just bounce off this suit and not touch you. So imagine yourself now wearing this suit. No one can see it but *you* know it is there. Imagine your boss making those critical comments in an unkind way – you hear the comments and see him saying them, yet you stay calm and keep smiling, as the words bounce off the suit. You're perfectly relaxed inside it. Those remarks just don't get to you anymore. You stay calm, relaxed and in control, and you handle the situation as *you* choose, instead of the way *he* chooses. You can just ignore the comments or you can say something appropriate, but not inflammatory. How he has spoken to you is *his* problem. He is out of control. You are *in* control. When your boss says things to you in a way designed to wind you up, you stay calm and relaxed and deal with the situation in an appropriately mature way."

After making these suggestions, Joe guided her back to enjoy the scenery and the blustery seashore once more, before counting back from 20 to 1 and inviting her to open her eyes again, feeling refreshed and alert. At the next session, Glenys joyfully reported that, although her boss had tried repeatedly to upset her with his criticism, she had ceased to respond. He was dumbfounded and, she thought, somewhat disappointed. But he now seemed to be treating her with a new and welcome respect.

Separate yourself from your anger

Despite what you or others may think, you are *not* an angry person. As we explained in Part 1, none of us carries anger inside us. Yes, you may be vulnerable to anger, quick to anger, prone to anger, or anger may even engulf you at times. But it does not naturally live inside you and it isn't a part of your personality – although, if you suffer from chronic anger because of high stress, it may seem to you as if it is, because you spend so much of the time feeling wound up.

If you have tried any of the techniques for lowering arousal that we have mentioned so far, you should have had the experience of feeling calmer and more relaxed, even if only for a short period. That serves to remind you of what it feels like to be without anger and that anger is *not* an intrinsic part of you.

> **❝ ... anger is _not_ an intrinsic part of you. ❞**

Many perceived injustices may arouse our anger. But anger can only take us over if we invite it to, however unintentionally, through the thoughts we choose to think and the scenarios we choose to imagine.

When you look at anger as something *outside* of yourself or reframe an anger-inducing event, you are using your thinking brain – your 'observing self' – and that keeps you calm and prevents the excitable emotional brain from getting caught up in the anger. You prevent yourself from engaging with anger and taking on its clothes. So, instead of thinking, "Why am I getting so angry?", try something like, "What can I do to stop anger taking a hold of me right now?" or "I refuse to let anger get to me". Be interested to see what effect that has on your arousal levels.

> **Anger can only take us over if we invite it to.**

Many people find it useful to make this understanding more concrete by giving their anger an imaginary form of some sort. For instance, one client chose to think of it as a bright red flame, which she then saw herself putting out by smothering with a cloth, to starve it of oxygen. Another imagined it as a grenade in his pocket and saw himself removing it quickly to a place of safety, carefully keeping the pin in place. Others opt for a coloured shape that symbolises anger for them. And some may choose a sound, like a car alarm or siren, which they imagine switching off, or even a bad smell, like rotting flesh, or an uncomfortable texture, like sandpaper, which they replace with a pleasant one.

EXERCISE: What represents anger for you?

See if you can come up with a powerful image or sensation that, for you, could represent your experience of anger. Then imagine deactivating it in whatever way seems appropriate. Now take a few moments to sit calmly. After a while, allow a little anger to arise in you by thinking of something that usually winds you up. Go for something general and relatively mild, such as being kept hanging on the line for ages when you telephone a company, or getting list after list of 'options' to choose from via the buttons on your handset, before getting through to a real live person. Next, practise bringing your chosen image or sensation to mind and deactivating it, as a means of letting go of the anger. If it works well for you, be ready to use it in a real situation. (If you find it doesn't, do some 7/11 breathing instead, to get your emotional arousal back down.)

Uncouple unhelpful pattern matches

If you spend a lot of time in a state of anger or anxiety, your brain's alarm system (the amygdala) is working overtime. And the more hyper-aroused you are about all sorts of things, the more it registers them as life-threatening events. Then, whenever it thinks that something similar is happening again, it sets the panic button off.

However, as we know, the amygdala is not a sophisticated organ. It often does the equivalent of 'cry wolf'. But, because we're not aware that this is what's happening, we behave as though it *is* a real wolf every time – and, to our emotional brain, it is. But we also have access to the higher brainpower of our rational mind, so it's important that we use this to supply the amygdala with better information.

So, if you find yourself beginning to react in a way that is completely out of proportion to the situation you are in, immediately set about calming yourself down with 7/11 breathing (or one of the other techniques we have suggested) and see if you can identify what your amygdala might be pattern matching to. In Part 1, we saw how Neil punched a doctor's receptionist in the face because his amygdala had patterned matched her long red hair to that of his former girlfriend, who betrayed and belittled him. But had Neil been able to calm himself down *before* he got physical, he would have had access to his thinking mind and his 'observing self', and so might have made the connection with his ex-girlfriend. "Of course! It's her hair! It's just like Janet's – *that's* what's winding me up. This woman is just doing her job. She isn't being rude."

Many years ago, Ivan was consulted by Vince, a seemingly quiet and pleasant young man. However, as Vince explained with some embarrassment, he often badly lost his temper with his partner Charlotte. He had never actually hit her but he feared he might. He had no idea why this was happening, as he adored Charlotte and they had a very happy life together.

Ivan soon discovered that the occasions on which Vince was most likely to become enraged were when Charlotte did something like tidying away his things when they had been left on the table ("But I know she is only making room to lay the table for dinner") or didn't agree with a suggestion he had made. Gradually it emerged that, as a young boy, Vince had felt very much undermined by his mother. She considered that she had the right to enter his room whenever she wanted and shift his belongings about as she pleased, or even to throw away whatever she thought had no further use. She would cook him bubble and squeak, even though she knew he loathed it, would buy 'family' chocolates that she knew his brother liked but that he didn't, failed to ask – or else ignored – his opinion on family matters, and generally treated him as if his views were of no consequence. Quickly Vince began to see that, when Charlotte did something that *seemed* to undermine him, he was reacting as if to his mother.

> **❝ ... our emotional brain makes crude pattern matches between past and present events. ❞**

"But why would I do that?" said Vince. "I know Charlotte is nothing like my mother!" Ivan explained that, rationally, Vince knew that but that his amygdala didn't. He told Vince about how the amygdala crudely pattern matches events in the present to events that have been highly threatening in the past and sets off the alarm to take action – fight or flight. As a boy, Vince had been fearful; as an adult, he became angry.

Ivan explained that, if we look for *similarities*, we find them. What Vince needed to do was look for *dissimilarities*, he said. So he asked Vince to go home and write a list of 50 ways that

Charlotte was different from his mother. Getting Vince's thinking brain to do the work of focusing on dissimilarities would put a stop to the 'thoughtless' pattern matching of the emotional brain. Vince duly came back with a long list of differences, such as "she supports me in what I do", "she values my opinion", "she is gentle and loving", "she only cooks meals we both like", "she never insults me", "she respects my need to be alone sometimes", etc. Ivan then asked him to read through his list every day for a week, so as to embed it in his consciousness, reminding him of how truly different Charlotte's behaviour was from that of his mother's. The more he did so, the less often he became angry and the pattern was broken.

As we have already seen, it isn't always possible to identify pattern matches, however, because, when they arise from a highly traumatic experience, elements of the pattern match may be unconscious (as happened in the case of Denny). In such cases, detraumatisation through the rewind technique is the best way to deal with the problem.

Remind yourself of what you've got going for you

People who get angry because low self-esteem makes them feel vulnerable will very often pattern match to past put-downs or to what they perceive are their failings. For instance, if they once got a question wrong in a maths class, and were laughed at by their class mates, they may become angry in the future, if asked a question they cannot answer. If a past girl-friend or boyfriend has let them down, then any new one will do the same. In other words, if they have ever unsuccessfully experienced anything remotely similar in the past, that will be what their amygdala latches on to.

EXERCISE: List your successes

If you recognise yourself in the above description, one good way to help break this pattern is to list your successes. List the times when you did have successful relationships, however long they lasted. Note down any time you remember doing well at school. There will no doubt be many forgotten occasions when you successfully faced challenging situations. Taking the time to recall them will bring them to the fore and make them more likely to become positive pattern matches for you in future.

Perhaps you are currently out of a job and don't have a relationship at the moment. If this is the case, it's important to remind yourself of all the jobs you have successfully held in the past, the qualifications you may have gained, the skills you have learned which enable you to do those jobs, and so forth. Count it as a resource if you have had boyfriends or girl-friends in the past, because that shows that you *are* capable of making a relationship work; if your marriage has broken down, still count it as a resource if, for a good part of the time, it worked well and you and your partner were happy.

However, if your instant response to the above suggestion was "I don't have *any* successes", you are in the grip of the black-and-white thinking we talked about earlier. So take some deep relaxing breaths and think again.

Next, list your abilities. We all have a variety of skills, experiences and attributes that we have developed and accumulated throughout our lives, and these, too, are resources we can draw on. But, when we are in a state of negative thinking, we may easily take some of them for granted, or forget them or even deny them. For instance, being able to carry out responsibilities, however minor, behaving caringly towards even one other person (whether a partner, a child, friend, relative or neighbour), enjoying hobbies – these all represent important traits and talents that we can build on.

So, be thorough. Write a list of *everything* you've got going for you. No skill is too small. Reminding yourself of your resources like this will help you to access them more easily, build your confidence and think more positively and productively about the future.

> 66 There will no doubt be many forgotten occasions when you successfully faced challenging situations. 99

Learn better ways to communicate

One of the prime reasons that people lose their cool is that they take exception to the way they are being spoken to. How we speak to others – whether those dearest to us, those we work with or those who work in places we often go to, such as shops, ticket offices and restaurants – communicates a great deal about how we think or feel about them. It can either inflame a difficult situation or calm it down.

In his training seminar on anger management,* Joe recommends his LIFE model of effective communication.

LIFE = Listening

Active listening, which we mentioned in Part 1, is a powerful skill we can all learn. It means listening to the other person without interrupting or giving advice, and then summarising back to them what you think you have heard, so that they know they have been heard correctly. If you have misunderstood something, they have the chance to set you right.

So, if someone is angry or upset ...

Let them emotionally unload, saying nothing but showing, by your expression or slight nods of the head, that you are attending (and *do* attend!) to what they are saying. Don't interrupt or challenge them, even if they are angry with you and

*This seminar is run by MindFields College. For more details, visit: www.mindfields.org.uk

what you are hearing about yourself is, you think, blatantly untrue. Always remember that, when we are emotionally aroused, the higher part of our brain shuts down and we can't think straight. We go into black-and-white, all-or-nothing mode ("you *never* do that", "you *always* do this"), so reality gets distorted.

Let's say that Anne's 14-year-old daughter Karen wants to go to a party at her friend Izzy's house. Anne doesn't know Izzy and has a strong suspicion that her parents could be away that weekend, as Karen has been rather evasive on that point. From an overheard conversation, Anne also suspects that some older boys might be coming over, who, quite possibly, could bring alcohol and drugs. So she tells Karen she can't go to the party. This opens the floodgates to a torrent of unkind accusations from Karen.

"You are the cruellest mother in the whole world! You've never cared about me, or what I want! Just because you had a miserable, boring childhood, you want to ruin mine too! You are so selfish and mean and horrible!"

Anne listens to this without flinching. She knows she must stay in her 'observing self', gathering information, not taking it personally and getting upset. She knows that Karen doesn't really mean what she is saying when she is upset like this. Her emotional brain is talking, not the real Karen. When her daughter has finished, Anne says, "If I understand you right,

Anger control and Asperger's syndrome

AS WE saw in Part 1 (on page 60), people with Asperger's syndrome typically feel a need for an ordered environment around them so that they can control things. This is because the uncertain nature of everyday life makes them highly anxious. As a result, they may well come across as 'control freaks', who insist on everything being done according to their own wishes and in their own favoured way. Although they may find it harder than other people to express warm emotion, they certainly don't lack emotion. Indeed, they are particularly vulnerable to emotional angry outbursts, when they get frustrated. They may be well aware that they are behaving tyrannically towards a partner or a colleague but they just can't stop themselves. Often, they say, "It just hits me so fast, I can't do a thing about it," or, "it's like having an out-of-control, wild animal inside me".

Some of the techniques so far described in this part of the book work better than others for people with Asperger's syndrome. For instance, we have found that people with Asperger's usually prefer to focus on the techniques that enable them to have full access to, and make full use of, the rational part of their brains – which, of course, shuts down almost completely when we are highly emotionally aroused. However, they tend to find it harder to engage with guided imagery, despite having good imaginations, and may not 'connect' with empowering suggestions put to them, while relaxed.

If you think you have Asperger traits, we suggest you try the following method of calming yourself down when you get highly emotionally aroused.

▶

Karen, you are saying that I'm being very cruel and uncaring towards you and that, because you think I had an unhappy childhood myself, I'm taking it out on you, through jealousy. I don't want you to have a good time and I'm a selfish and mean mother."

Karen will probably be stunned when she hears this said to her in a calm tone. But it may spur her to add some more insults and criticisms. If she does, Anne will summarise those

- Once you are aware that you have 'lost it', do anything that will give you 'time out' to calm down. Put down the phone if you have become abusive. Or walk out of the room, telling your partner you are going out for a while to 'cool off'.

- Separate yourself from the anger. Imagine your emotional arousal as a wild, untamed animal. It helps to see that spitting, flailing animal as not the real 'you'.

- Do intensive 7/11 breathing to bring your arousal down or do something highly physical, such as running or circuit training.

- Once you have lowered your emotional arousal and enabled the thinking brain to get a look in, use it to let you take a wider perspective. For instance, write down what the wild animal was telling you ("It's not fair!" "I won't be treated like this!" "Who *does* she think she is?") and question those assumptions. Put yourself in the other person's shoes. Were they really meaning to be unkind? To be disrespectful? Or ▶

too. Instead of giving Karen's emotional brain more fuel (in the form of shouting back) to keep its arousal going, doing the summarising will start to calm it down. Karen's thinking brain can then start to get a look in and can consider the content of the words that are being summarised back.

So Karen, at some point, will probably say, "Well, I don't actually mean that you are the cruellest mum in the world or that you don't care about me or never let me do anything nice,

patronising? Do you really expect to control *everything*? Or was it the wild animal, raring up and baring its teeth, that was acting that way?

■ The more you question, the more you are taming that wild animal inside you. And, the more often you do this, the weaker the wild animal will become. As you gain power over it and more awareness, you may also begin to recognise some of the warning signals that indicate you are about to blow – feeling hot and sweaty, perhaps, or starting to want to clench your fists or move your legs, or feeling a blinding pain in your head. Then whenever you spot such a warning sign, take time out immediately and work your way through all the points above.

■ The more you question the wild animal's behaviour and motives – in a civilised society, should we really be behaving like wild animals, fighting to get our own way, regardless of the consequences to anyone else? – the less powerful and driving they will become.

but I do want to go to this party. And I do think you are being cruel!" This is a definite climb-down from the original position and, in this frame of mind, Karen is clearly able to weigh up information.

At this point, then, Anne can give her own view. "It's because I do care about you that I can't let you go to this party. You are only 14 and it is still my job to protect you, and I think the risks of this party getting out of hand, even though you have nothing to do with that, are just too great to take. I fully accept you don't agree – and, as your parent, I have to take the action I think is appropriate."

Karen still won't be happy, of course, and she may still make a point of stamping out and slamming a door. But the heat has cooled and Karen knows that her viewpoint has been heard, if not shared.

Active listening is a really meaningful way of expressing caring for another person. If you listen actively, you are showing that you are prepared to suspend judgement and make the effort to empathise with and understand what the other person is feeling, even if they are being critical and hurtful towards you. You are affirming their right to their feelings, however much those may differ from yours. That is truly a demonstration of emotional generosity and it transforms relationships between parents and children, and between couples.

LIFE = I, not you

Grievances commonly escalate into rows because we accuse other people of doing or not doing things we don't like, instead of starting from how whatever we are aggrieved about is making us feel.

Instead of screaming, "You never clear away the breakfast things and wash up!", your point is much more likely to be heard if you say something like, "I feel upset and angry when I come home from a long day's work and find your breakfast things still on the table and none of it washed up."

When we blame, the other person gets upset and defensive, even if they know they are in the wrong. But when we speak from the 'I' position, we are not attacking anyone; we are just describing the circumstances that explain or justify our feelings.

Speaking from the 'I' instead of the 'you' position is routinely recommended in assertiveness training courses. But here we part company with them, because they usually suggest at this point that, in effect, you tell the other person what to do that will put the situation right. For example, "I appreciate that you are also in a rush to get to school. However, I would like to come home to a clean, tidy kitchen."

This sounds reasonable enough. But the risk in doing that is that you are removing the other person's chance to take some control over the situation. (And, as you may recall, having a degree of control over what we do is one of our fundamental emotional needs.) So the effect of taking this approach may well be that the person becomes resentful or defensive again. If, instead, you stop at the point where you have described and explained your feelings, the other person has the chance to make a contribution towards solving the problem. They can *choose* to wash up and put the breakfast things away. And, if they do, they will also be more likely to do it in future than if the solution was imposed on them.

LIFE = Freedom to own our own problems

If someone else's behaviour is adversely affecting you in some way, you have a problem that needs sorting out. But you do not have a problem if their circumstances or behaviour are not affecting you (or are not causing a risk which, as a parent or citizen, you have a duty to act to prevent). It makes no difference whether you don't like what is happening or you are upset on the other person's behalf. It is best, on such occasions, to stay out of the matter and think of what is happening as a 'developmental opportunity' for the person concerned. After all, if you rush in to solve every problem, you are denying people their opportunity to develop by working out how to handle it for themselves. Only if our help is asked for should we become involved in the problem-solving process.

Suppose little Dylan comes home from school, highly upset because his best friend made fun of him in class. His dad feels instinctively protective and wants to show him how to stand up for himself, perhaps even demonstrating some blocking moves, should it all come to blows. His mum, on the other hand, wants to phone the best friend's mother and talk it out with her. Both would be stealing Dylan's developmental opportunity!

The correct response is active listening: "It must be really upsetting having your best friend treat you like that." If, later, Dylan says to his mum or dad, "What would *you* do about it?", then it is acceptable to give advice.

Remember, advice that is unasked for is almost always seen as criticism. To the person with the problem it sounds as if you are saying, "Why on earth didn't you think of doing *this*, *this* or *this*?"

LIF**E** = Everyone's a winner!

When we are in conflict with others, our aim should be to come up with a solution that satisfies everyone, rather than leaving one person a winner and others the losers. Even if the solution feels good to the winner at the time, it is only a short-term triumph because relationships will suffer in the long run.

This is because arguments are not usually about who is wrong and who is right but about a clash of needs. In searching for solutions, therefore, we must look for what needs are not being met for the individuals concerned, and make sure the solution takes account of them.

For instance, Peter used to have to leave home before his young children were awake in order to make his long journey to his office. On most evenings, he returned after they were in bed, so he really looked forward to the one day a week on which he could get home early because he spent the afternoon on that day at a branch office close to his home. He would drive home, savouring the prospect of catching up with his children, playing a game with them and just generally hanging out with them. But he couldn't fail to notice that, lately, instead of running to the door to greet him, they didn't acknowledge him at all. They stayed glued to some television programme.

Peter could easily have pulled fatherly rank by storming into the room, turning off the television and saying to them loudly, "I think I deserve something better than this on the one night I get home early! From now on, when you hear my car turn into the drive on a Wednesday evening, you make sure that television is switched off!"

Fortunately, Peter didn't choose to do that. He waited until the programme they were watching was over and then he called them over for a chat. "You know, I so look forward to spending time with you on the one evening I get home early. I feel really disappointed that, when I come in these days, you're always glued to the TV and hardly even notice I'm home. Is

The 'good argument' guide

IF YOU have a lot of arguments with your partner, it is not necessarily a sign of a bad relationship or that you are ill-suited. What matters is *how* you argue. American psychologist and relationship expert John Gottman has researched thousands of couples' relationships and found that arguing, even intensely, can be healthy if it airs grievances and complaints in a productive way, which enables them to be resolved. But when a difference of opinion descends into blaming, accusing, generalising, exaggerating and undermining each other's character, then arguing *isn't* healthy – and, according to Gottman's findings, the relationship is unlikely to survive.

So, if you have a difference of opinion you want to thrash out with anyone, not just your partner, here's how to keep the argument healthy:

■ agree to have five minutes each to speak without interruption

■ stick to the issue under discussion; do not bring up grievances from the past ("Three years ago, when I wanted us to visit my mother that time, you …!")

■ do not attack each other's character ("You lying toe-rag!" "You've always been a shifty good-for-nothing!")

■ avoid the words 'always' and 'never'; this is unlikely to be true

■ when the first person has spoken, the second should summarise what they think was said, without judgement or criticism. The first speaker then corrects their summary, if necessary

▶

there something we can do about this, I wonder?" And he left the problem with them and went upstairs for a shower.

When he came back down, one of the children said, "Daddy, we've been thinking. Why don't we record that cartoon programme we love? Then we can play with you when you get in and watch it after dinner."

Peter was happy and the children were happy. Everyone's needs were met.

■ then the second person speaks for five minutes, after which the first person summarises (again without blame or criticism) and the speaker corrects as necessary

■ say nothing more at this point! Agree to go away and digest what you have heard, whether you agree with it or not

■ if there is something to be resolved, agree to meet again later or the next day, at a specified time, and use the same rules (no blaming, no character assassination, no interrupting, etc.) to put forward and discuss possible solutions. Do not use language secretly designed to antagonise or demean. For instance, if one person has superior reasoning skills and can rebut with ease each point the other makes, the one who feels thwarted is eventually left with only an emotional response possible – "You *******!" Remember, if there is a dispute, it is because there is a clash of needs. So it is important genuinely to value each other's contribution and to find out what each person's needs are. ●

The painkillers

Another example of this occurred when a colleague of ours was on holiday in Spain with her husband and they were setting off to stay for a weekend with old friends, who now lived in that country. Their holiday cottage was on the outskirts of a small town, and they had to drive through the centre of it to gain access to the motorway. The town was always full of traffic during the day and it could take 20 minutes or more to get through it. When they were halfway out of the town, her husband, who was suffering from severe pain as a result of a back injury, remembered that he had forgotten to bring with him his strong prescription painkillers. Our colleague was all for returning to get them, knowing that he would have a terrible night's sleep that night, and would not only be in avoidable pain but would be irritable the next day – which might lead to unnecessary unpleasantness with their friends. But he was adamant that he would not go back, unwilling to face the prospect of re-negotiating the traffic jams, and she knew better than to push the point.

Noticing that petrol was low, her husband suggested pulling into the petrol station before going on the motorway. Our colleague saw her chance. She was the one carrying the foreign currency and, as she genuinely hadn't expected that they would be getting petrol, she was now concerned that they didn't have enough money with them to pay their way comfortably over the weekend (they had been planning to take their friends out for a meal).

"It's a shame to spoil the weekend for the sake of 40 euros," she said. "Why don't we go back to get some more money and pick up your painkillers at the same time?"

Now that they would be returning not just because of his forgetfulness but to collect the extra money that they might need, her husband was willing to return home, traffic or not. He was happy because he had saved face and also got his painkillers. She was happy because, free of pain, he could enjoy the weekend – and she didn't have to worry about him losing his temper over any minor irritation which might be blown out of proportion through the combination of a poor night's sleep and persistent pain.

What if there is no win–win?

In some situations, of course, someone has to give way. But, if each person's position is considered with equal respectfulness by both parties, then it becomes possible for them to agree, on the basis of that information, whose needs have greater priority on that occasion.

For instance, Monica wants to watch her dance programme on the television. Dave wants to watch a football match on the sports channel. Although they have two televisions, one is a little portable in the bedroom and the other is a large, high quality one in the living room. Both, therefore, prefer to watch downstairs. But the sports channel is only connected to the television in the living room so, when Dave wants to watch his sport, he *has* to watch downstairs. As Dave enjoys watching a lot of sport, this understandably irks Monica, as she is always the one relegated to the portable upstairs. Having listened to each other's points of view, they have decided that, when it is an important match, Dave will have the television downstairs; when the programme Monica wants to see is an absolute favourite of hers, she will be the one to watch downstairs. If the two conflict, on one occasion Monica will tape her programme and watch it downstairs later and, on the next occasion, Dave will go out to watch his match in a pub, if he wants to see it live. The system keeps them both happy.

Sometimes, of course, one person will have to give way altogether – for instance, if a couple plan to go to the cinema but want to see different films. In that event, it is helpful if, rather than resenting it, the person who gives way regards it as an investment in the relationship, which builds good will for the next time a choice has to be made.

Working with consequences

But there will be times when negotiation just does not seem to work. Suppose you have tried everything described above and your son still refuses to put any real effort into looking for a job, or your daughter still leaves her clothes lying in a heap any old where, or perhaps your partner still continues to come home late on the one night you have a babysitter and can go out together. In such cases, it is time to introduce the understanding that, if such behaviour continues, there will be consequences. However, 'consequences' is not another word for punishment; nor does it mean threat. It means that, if the same old same old happens yet again, you will be taking a particular action. These consequences need to be explained clearly beforehand, so that the other person has the chance to choose whether to change their behaviour or to accept the consequences. And, of course, you *have* to stick to the plan and carry out the consequences *every time* you establish them. Otherwise, the idea of consequences won't be taken seriously and won't ever work.

Ivan once suggested to a woman, who was almost at breaking point when she came to see him for help, that she try using consequences. Fran was over-stressed by the various demands of her life and anxious and angry about her son Steve's refusal to work for his exams. He was a talented tennis player and, to give him a chance to pursue his dream, she and her husband were paying for him to go to a tennis school, where he could also study for his A-levels. To be able to do

How to prevent children's tantrums

■ Make sure you give attention to and comment positively on the little things that your children do right (for instance, when young children button their coats correctly, carry a full cup without spilling anything, remember to brush their teeth, or when older children wash up, clear up after themselves or do neat homework). Also comment positively on efforts they make, even if the results aren't yet perfect. This way, children learn to value themselves and to want to please, and have less need to seek attention through bad behaviour or incessant demands.

■ Apply your LIFE skills. When children want something they cannot have, use active listening skills and encourage them to come up with alternative options. Be respectful of all their suggestions and think them through together – even young children will be able to see when their ideas are not workable, once they feel their ideas have been listened to and explored.

■ Make sure children know your rules (for instance, no sweets after school or no staying up after 7 pm on school-days) and stick to them. Check they know what the rules are *before* you reach crisis point (the sweet shop looms; the clock strikes seven etc.), not afterwards. ●

this, she had had to go back to work full time, instead of part time, and was finding it highly stressful trying to do a demanding job with long hours and keep the house and family going. Added to this, her husband worked away for long stretches of time, so wasn't able to play much part in sorting out domestic affairs. Fran continually asked Steve to help with some of the household chores, to lighten her load, but he always refused, none too politely. Whenever she pointed out that she was in her current stressful situation because of trying to help him have his chance to progress in tennis, he would typically say, "You know I'm grateful for that but you getting stressed over it has nothing to do with me. And I don't care if the place is clean and tidy, so why should I do any cleaning? You're the one who is bothered about it. So *you* do it."

Understandably, Fran was upset by his response. She was also upset by the fact that Steve wasn't bothering to work for his exams. "I've nagged and I've nagged, but he won't do a thing, unless it suits him. In fact, he is doing even less than before!" The upshot of all this was that Fran and Steve were locked in endless arguments and shouting matches.

Ivan pointed out to her that, by nagging, she was in effect trying to control Steve's behaviour and so Steve's instinctive response, to regain control, was to do the opposite of whatever she was suggesting. The first priority now, he said, was for Fran to bring her own stress levels down and she could do that by setting out very clearly to Steve their situation and what was going to happen next.

"Tell him calmly that you feel deeply frustrated, angry and hurt about his unwillingness to do anything to lessen your load, when you have taken on the burden of full-time work purely for his sake, and are struggling under the stress of it. Tell him that, if he is not willing to meet you halfway, there will be consequences. Say that, as part of the problem is that he leaves his clothing strewn over the floor in his room and doesn't put the dirty clothes in the laundry basket for washing, you will no longer go in there to sort it all out for him. And, if he doesn't do the chores you ask, you will do no laundry or ironing for him.

"Also point out that, at the rate he is going on, he is unlikely to get the grades he needs to go to university and neither can he depend on his tennis. Remind him that all his friends will be going to university and that, if his tennis doesn't work out, he'll be left stuck at home, with only some dead-end job to look forward to. Then say that you won't mention the matter again. It is his life and he will reap whatever he chooses to sow."

Fran later found a suitable moment when she could talk calmly to Steve and duly told him all this. Angrily, he marched out of the room and slammed the door. He made no changes to his behaviour, so Fran stopped doing his washing. At first, Steve didn't care. But, when he ran out of clean clothes, he started having to wear again the ones he had discarded. Although Fran found it hard to stick to her word – it was unpleasant for her and everyone else when he walked around in clothes that were becoming increasingly stained and smelly, and she was also embarrassed for him – her annoyance at Steve's behaviour sustained her and she didn't give in. Some weeks later, he asked her how to use the washing machine and the iron. She was thrilled! At least, he was now taking care of two time-consuming tasks.

> 66 That had the added bonus of stopping all the endless arguments. 99

For the first two weeks after their initial conversation, Steve did no schoolwork whatsoever. Clearly, he was testing her. But Fran stayed firm, difficult for her though it was, and said nothing. That had the bonus effect of stopping the endless arguments. And because Steve was now much calmer, instead of being in a constant state of rebellion, he soon came to realise that most of his friends *were* now studying hard and were full of their plans for the future. So he started to study, too. This soon brought praise from his teachers (as well as his mother) instead of criticism and, as he found he liked that, he kept on with the studying.

He didn't become a model child, but he had learned some important lessons – and life at home was less stressful all round.

Come up with something suitable

It is best to try to come up with consequences that are directly related to the behaviour you are looking for, rather than
something random, such as stopping pocket money or, in the
case of a partner, withholding sex – both of which come across
as more like punishments anyway. The consequence also
needs to be one that you know you can enforce. It is no good
saying to a teenage son, "In that case, you are not going out!"

> **Consequences
> give you a measure
> of control over the
> situation ...**

if he is inches taller and kilos heavier
than you and you couldn't realistically
stop him leaving the house, if he were
determined to.

Your aim, instead, is to enlist co-
operation. Michael's daughter thought-
lessly went off to school leaving her radio still blaring out
music in her room. Every day, Michael had to climb three
flights of stairs to her attic bedroom to switch if off before
leaving for work. So one day he said to her, "I'm fed up with
this! If I have to go all the way up to your room once more to
turn the radio off, I will remove the plug. I am not doing this
to punish you, just to make you pay attention to what you
need to do. My feeling is that, if you have to come downstairs
every day to get the plug and put it back on the radio, you will
stop forgetting to turn the radio off."

He was right.

If the behaviour of a partner, colleague, friend or family member is unacceptable to you and they are not amenable to discussing or altering it, you will cease to feel so frustrated if you state how you plan to act, as a consequence, and stick to it. "You know I don't like Ian. I don't like it when you bring him home with you, automatically expecting he can stay for a meal, and you both end up drinking a lot. It always leads to an argument between you and me later. You say you won't tell him not to come. So, in future, if you turn up with him, I won't be cooking and I shall leave and stay at mum's for the night."

You are, in effect, exerting a measure of control over the situation, instead of feeling disempowered, even if you can't get the exact outcome you would ideally like.

Why carrying through consequences is a kindness

SOMETIMES we may feel we are being unnecessarily hard, if we insist that children live by the consequences of their behaviour. In fact, we are doing them a kindness. If a child leaves their bike unlocked outside a shop, despite being told to use the padlock, and it is stolen, what do they learn if they are instantly bought a replacement bike? They learn that they don't have to bother to take care of their possessions. This is not a trait that will serve them well in life.

How to handle criticism or unreasonable requests

Nobody likes to be criticised or feel taken advantage of. If we use the methods of communication described in the LIFE system, we can reduce the likelihood of hurting other people and/or making them angry.

But, of course, we can't control how people talk to *us*! So, if we are the ones who feel criticised or taken advantage of, we need to find ways to defuse the other person's frustration or anger, and to stop resentment and anger building up in ourselves. Here are some effective techniques for doing this.

Fogging

The idea here is that you create a 'fog' so that someone who is trying to get at you and hurt you can't actually find you as a target. One way to do this, when on the receiving end of criticism, is to agree with an aspect of it that *is* true. There usually is at least an element of truth in criticisms that are levelled at us but what usually gets to us and makes us cross is that it is exaggerated and blown out of all proportion. So, to the criticism that "You think you're so clever and that you know more about why I'm behaving the way I'm behaving than I do!", one response (if applicable) might be: "It's true I studied psychology and it's true that that doesn't necessarily mean that I know more about behaviour than anyone else." This takes the wind out of the accuser's sails because you have acknowledged two truths without actually agreeing with their point, but also without contradicting it.

If you can't agree with the truth of the statement itself, you can always find something else to agree with:

- *"You may be right"* (it is no more than a possibility).
- *"You may well be right"* (it's certainly a possibility).
- *"You have a point"* (I think it is a stupid one but it is a point and it's yours!).

Accept mistakes

Remember that the intensity of our emotional conviction is no sure guide to the accuracy of our perception, or memory of an event. In Part 1, we described how emotional arousal stops our brains from functioning at their best. So, when we get wound up about something, we are least likely to be certain of our ground. Mum: "You said that you would clear that mess up after dinner!" Son: "I didn't say that! I didn't make that mess!" Mum: "You did!" Son: "I didn't!" Mum: "You were standing right there, by that chair, when you said, 'I'll clear this up as soon as we've had dinner'!" Son: "I've just come downstairs. I wasn't standing by that chair. It was Graham who was down here, not me."

Suddenly, mum remembers it was her other son, Graham, who had made the mess. She can now refuse to back down, in an ill-advised attempt to save face: "Well, you're just as bad as him, anyway. If it hadn't been him, it would have been you!" Or she can accept her mistake: "Oh, I'm so sorry! I got it wrong. I apologise, darling." The first response is likely to lose her respect from her son; the second is likely to earn it because, when we have been vindicated, we can always afford to be magnanimous.

We all make mistakes at times, especially when we are tired or emotional or are trying to deal with too many things at once. We don't have to feel guilty about making them, however, if we take responsibility for our mistakes and, where appropriate, learn from them and do what we can to put them right.

Disclose a personal 'failing'

Imagine this scenario. Your neighbour bangs urgently on the door. "Please lend me your car for half an hour. My mother-in-law's got to get to her hair appointment and she's left it too late to get the bus. In fact, we'll be cutting it fine even by car, now. She'll be heartbroken if she can't get it done today as she's going out tonight. I can't take mine because it's in for repairs after that accident I had last week. But I promise I'll drive yours really carefully! I'm insured to drive any car."

Perhaps you are thinking to yourself, "If his mother-in-law really wanted to get her hair done so much, why didn't she make sure she left enough time to make her way there? And, if they are almost late already, they're going to have to drive very fast – in my car. And he's already had an accident which, I happen to know, was caused because he was driving too fast!"

You do not want to lend your car. You also do not want to open the floodgates to his consequent rage and frustration and make an enemy of him for life. So you might decide to say something like this:

"I would so like to help. But I have this thing where I get ridiculously anxious about my car. When I've lent it in the past, I almost get panic attacks, I'm so worried. It's ridiculous, I know, but I can't help it. It's nothing to do with your driving. It's me. I'm so sorry I can't help." The chances are that your neighbour will go away bewildered and a little sorry for you – but not angry.

How to handle unreasonable demands

There are always occasions, just like that described above, when people try to push us into doing something we don't want to do. Either we say no and they get angry with us or we give in, and suffer huge resentment ourselves. The 'broken record technique' is an excellent way to deflect unreasonable demands without emotional fall-out. Here's how it works.

Matt is an extremely hardworking deputy manager. He willingly puts himself out for his rather selfish boss, although he doesn't get much in the way of thanks for it, and feels his boss often tries to take too much advantage. After learning the broken record technique, however, he now feels much more in control.

One afternoon, at about 4 o'clock, his boss came into his room and said, "I'm going to have to ask you to stay late tonight, Matt. I know it's short notice but I have to get all those figures ready for tomorrow's meeting and I'm behind with them."

Matt is meeting a friend from out of town for an early supper – the friend must start her journey home mid-evening. He hasn't seen his friend for two years and both are really looking forward to catching up. Thankfully Matt remembers the broken record technique.

"I would really like to help you, Chris, but I'm meeting up with an old friend from out of town tonight and so have to leave work at the normal time."

At this Chris says, "Oh, Matt, this is so important! It's a key meeting. Couldn't you cancel it?"

"I know it's important to you. However, I'm meeting up with a friend from out of town tonight whom I haven't seen for a long time and so I have to leave work at the normal time."

"It will do a lot for your chances of a pay rise, if you stay tonight. I'll put in a good word!"

"I appreciate your offer to show your gratitude in that way. However, I am meeting up with a friend from out of town tonight and so I have to leave work at the normal time."

"Don't you care about the mauling I'm going to get at the

meeting, if I look unprepared?"

"I do want you to be able to do your best at the meeting tomorrow and I'm prepared to drop everything to help you right now. However, I am meeting up with a friend from out of town tonight and so I have to leave work at the normal time."

If you do not get caught up in answering or defending yourself against whatever the other person tries to throw at you, and you stick with repeating your position as Matt did, like a broken record, you have a far higher chance of getting your way without causing antagonism.

> 66 The 'broken record technique' is an excellent way to deflect unreasonable demands... 99

The broken record technique can also be tried when *you* are the one seeking the favour or wanting to get your point across. In such circumstances, you just keep acknowledging the responses made to you and repeating your own position, in the same way as above. It doesn't *always* work, of course, so use it sparingly!

How to protect yourself from violence at work

Nowadays, many people who work with the public find themselves under threat of violence every day – from angry passengers, patients, customers and so on. It is crucial, therefore, to know how to defuse such terrifying situations, rather than exacerbate them.* The advice that follows can also be useful in other situations where a person is displaying uncontrolled anger – for instance, over a parking space they think they have a right to or some accidental damage you may have caused.

If we want to stop someone from attacking us, we need them to perceive us, in their emotional brains, as being on their side, and therefore not an enemy. Remember, when someone is angry with you, they are highly emotionally aroused and therefore only thinking in black-and-white terms. At that moment, you are not an individual to them. You are a representative of the system or just a suitable receptacle for their rage, because, as far as they are concerned, you are either with them or against them: you are part of the solution or part of the problem. So, to make them feel that we are on their side, we need to step inside their model of reality and understand how they are feeling. We must do nothing that makes them think

* If you work in any of the public services, dealing directly with the public, and want detailed advice on coping with angry customers, patients and clients, we recommend *Managing the Monkey: how to defuse the conflicts that can lead to violence in the workplace* by Mark Dawes with Denise Winn (HG Publishing, RRP £9.99).

either that we are patronising them or else that we are taking them on. This means being very careful with any efforts to build rapport with them, which is what we naturally do, when trying to relate successfully with someone.

Tread a fine line between matching and mismatching

Rapport building is a basic key skill in building relationships. We can't form relationships unless we feel that the other person likes/trusts or gets on with us and vice versa. At its most basic level, good rapport is achieved through a 'dance' of matching movements – we adopt the same body positions, the same facial expressions, the same tone of voice and the same speed of speech as the person we are communicating with. When people are in rapport, they unconsciously move into positions that mirror each other's. If you look around a bar, couples and friends that are clearly enjoying each other's company will usually *both* have an elbow resting on the arm rest of their chairs or will *both* be leaning forward to each other, *both* with their legs crossed or uncrossed, and so on. We can turn this tendency to conscious advantage when we want to create rapport, for instance with a prospective employer, by deliberately mirroring the other person's behaviour. *However*, doing this with an extremely angry person is a completely different kettle of fish. If you lean towards them or clench your hands into fists like theirs or copy their nervous movements, they will, of course, think that you are getting ready for a fight with them – and that is the last thing you want.

> *You must only try to create rapport by matching someone's body movements if there is absolutely no risk that they can misinterpret your intentions.*

For instance, if the person is standing and you are sitting, slowly stand up. If they have both their hands placed on the far side of your desk, lightly place both of your hands on your side of the desk at some point during your response. What we don't want to do is create a mismatching of behaviours. If someone is ranting and raving at you, and you remain calmly seated, hands in your lap and looking anywhere but at your aggressor, you will appear completely disrespectful, and that will be like a red rag to a bull. But copying their aggressive moves, or what could be interpreted as aggressive moves, is *always* a no-no.

Highly experienced conflict management consultant Mark Dawes (author of the book mentioned at the bottom of page 178) advises that, when someone is coming angrily towards us, invading our personal space and looking seriously threatening, we should do what our instincts at once tell us to do: *take one step back*. That immediately signals to the other person that we do not plan to be aggressive but also that we are taking them seriously. Our next instinct is to protect our bodies and/or faces and we do this by raising our hands in front of us. Dawes advises we do this firmly, bringing the hands to chin level, palms forward. This is a placatory gesture, not a victim or aggressor one: it makes us feel a bit safer and, therefore, in a stronger position for defending ourselves.

Don't speak calmly

Have you ever been absolutely furious about something and the person to whom you are talking says to you, in a slow, calm voice, "Don't get yourself upset, now." As you are upset already, being talked to like that just increases your anger – you're obviously not getting through! When dealing with someone who is angry, therefore, not only do we need to avoid mismatching our behaviour with theirs, we also need to avoid a mismatch between tones of voice. So, if someone is raising their voice to you in anger, speak a little louder than usual (but don't shout). You should also speak a little more urgently than you would normally and – very importantly – the words you speak must not be critical. They must show instead that you genuinely appreciate what the person is experiencing. "I understand that you are extremely upset that our no-refund policy prevents us from giving you your money back!"

Mr Johnson's cancelled operation

Let us suppose that Mr Johnson has come to hospital for a routine operation. It has been cancelled three times already but this time it is going ahead. The hospital is quite a distance from his home, so he and his wife, who has come up with him, have had to put the dog in kennels for a week and both have arranged time off work. Mr Johnson is in reception, waiting to be taken up to the ward. A porter arrives with a wheelchair, ready to take him up, and rings the ward to see if they are ready. He then turns to Mr Johnson with a sympathetic shrug and says that he has just been told that an emergency has come in and Mr Johnson's operation has had to be cancelled again. He tells him to go to reception to re-schedule.

We can imagine how Mr Johnson is feeling right now. Already nervous about the operation, his arousal is sky-high. He charges towards the reception desk, apoplectic with rage, leans over the receptionist and starts to shout. "You can't *do* this! It's *outrageous*! It's completely out of order. Do you know what it's cost us to get here today, taking time off work and putting the dog into kennels? If a private company were run like this, it would be bankrupt. How *dare* you think you can treat me like this! I've waited ages for this operation."

The receptionist needs to stand up slowly, to create un-threatening matching of behaviour. Mr Johnson is angry but he is not imminently about to attack her, so she doesn't need

Five steps for calming aggression

THESE simple steps will help calm the situation down when people are angry about what they perceive as unjust treatment.

1. Feed back the person's request or complaint, to show that it has been correctly heard and that you empathise with their position. ("I can see that you are really upset that these errors have occurred on your account.") **This step is vital.** It is no good just offering to put a wrong right. You have to acknowledge the person's feelings first and show them that their upset has been fully registered.

2. Offer a statement of regret and sincere apology. ("I am so sorry that this has happened and has caused you such inconvenience/distress.") You are not taking responsibility by doing this; you are just expressing what should be genuine regret about the distress the problem has caused.

3. Acknowledge responsibility, if appropriate. ("It was human error"/ "our accounting system software had a glitch last week.") Do not avoid taking responsibility to save face or try to pass it off somewhere else.

4. Clearly state your wish to find a solution that will satisfy everyone. ("I will take steps to rectify this at once." "I will take steps straight away to find out what has happened here.")

5. Offer a compromise or remedy the complaint in some way. ("I will personally make sure that the incorrect statement is deleted from the system and a new, correct one issued to you tomorrow.") Do not say that you can do nothing. There is always something that can be offered to restore good will.

to adopt a defensive posture. But what she does next is vital for ensuring that his arousal doesn't escalate and the risk to her become acute. Speaking in a firm, slighter louder than normal voice, she must start with active listening: she must feed back Mr Johnson's complaint, to show that he has been heard and that she is taking it seriously.

"Mr Johnson, I fully understand that you are feeling furious! I would be, too, if my operation were cancelled four times! I want to see what I can do about this!" Importantly, this last statement explains her standing up, so that he doesn't misconstrue it as an attack. She has also entered his model of reality, by indicating that she would feel the same if treated as Mr Johnson has been treated.

Next, she needs to get Mr Johnson away from where he can present a threat to her. She doesn't want to be trapped behind the desk with him leaning over it. She wants him to sit down again in the public waiting area, while she tries to sort things out. She does *not* say, "Go and sit over there, please", as that would be like asking him to withdraw from the 'territory' he has just invaded and admit defeat. So instead, she says, "Mr Johnson, would you come with me, please" and both leave the 'territory' together. She walks fast, to reflect his agitated state, but keeps out of possible

> 66 This statement explains her standing up, so he doesn't misconstrue it as an attack. 99

punching distance. When they reach the public waiting area, she says, "Mr Johnson, would you sit here for a moment, please, while I just find out what we can do about this." It is now in Mr Johnson's interests to sit quietly and wait, as the receptionist is going off expressly to deal with his case. Having defused the immediate situation, and given Mr Johnson an opportunity to calm down, she then goes off to take advice/get help.

Take sensible physical precautions

- Wherever you work, make sure that you have an unimpeded escape route, if necessary. In a private office, for instance, don't have your desk facing the door, as that enables someone to corner you by standing on the other side of the desk, thus getting between you and the door. If possible, have a door behind you, which you can always escape through.

- Check that you don't leave possible weapons, such as scalpels, scissors or heavy paperweights lying in view and in reach.

- If someone is acting in a seriously aggressive way towards you and you feel extremely unsafe and at risk, don't waste time trying any calming down measures. Just give an excuse ("I'm going to go and get more information on this"/"I'll just get the file") and get straight out of the room. Don't go back (or certainly not alone). If the person gets fed up with waiting, they will leave. And, if they wreck your work area before they leave, that's annoying. But you are alive!

- Be aware that the risks don't only come from strangers. In these days of hugely increased work pressure, even stressed-out colleagues can suddenly lose it. Keep an eye on changes in behaviour, such as consistently turning up late for work, drinking more heavily or uncharacteristic emotional outbursts. These are danger signs that the person's behaviour could tip out of control, if they feel thwarted or suddenly vulnerable. Avoid being alone with them, whether in the office, the lift or the car park.

- Never get into a lift if, when it opens, someone already inside it makes you feel uncomfortable. Pretend you are waiting for someone and look away.

And remember, silence can be golden ...

Quite a lot of arguments or anger outbursts could be prevented if, sometimes, we kept our thoughts to ourselves. Not every irritation we experience needs to be communicated to the 'guilty party'. Some people will always leave their dirty plates lying around; or will throw rubbish at the rubbish bin, miss and leave it on the floor; or will make an annoying throat clearing noise when reading; or will hang their wet coat on top of your dry one. Sometimes, it is better to put up with whatever is annoying us, or take the necessary corrective action ourselves, than to get hot under the collar and have to 'have it out' with the person. Women usually have a greater physiological need to express their feelings than men do, but it is still worth biting your tongue at times, for the sake of peace and good will. (Try expressing any arousal you may feel through some quick physical action instead, such as running up and down stairs.)

Let the minor things go. And that *means* let them go – don't hold on to them and build up resentment. Save your negotiating skills for the things that really matter. It will change the atmosphere at home, with friends and in work relationships for the better, and there will be far

> 66 It will change the atmosphere at home, with friends and in work relationships for the better. 99

fewer arguments overall, because you cease to be perceived as a nag or too harsh a critic.

* * * * *

You may well find that the practical advice in this section is sufficient to help you bring about change to the angry behaviour that you find troublesome – whether it is yours or someone else's. But not everyone finds it easy to initiate major change without someone to give them extra guidance and support along the way – or perhaps you suspect that you need a little help to detraumatise something that's happened to you. Part 3 offers advice on how to find effective, professional help and gives you a glimpse of the variety of ways in which human givens therapists may work when clients come to them for help with anger.

Seeking professional help

---

*A*LTHOUGH many readers of this book may now feel
that they know what to do to regain control of their anger, not
everyone feels confident about getting to grips with new ideas
or putting into practice new techniques by themselves; some
of us want the support of someone who is highly experienced
in them already. Sometimes, too, we get 'tunnel vision', and
are capable of focusing on little other than our own narrow
problem writ large. At times like these, we need someone
else to help us put things back into proper perspective and to
offer the reframes that open us to the possibility of seeing our
circumstances in a different light.

And, as we have seen, if your anger has its root in high
emotional arousal due to a past traumatic event, this needs to
be resolved, so that the events can be processed as a normal
memory, without the attendant, incapacitating emotion. This
is best done by a therapist who is proficient in the rewind
technique, which we will describe shortly.

Choosing a therapist is an extremely important step. Incredible as it may seem, there are well over 400 schools of psychotherapy and counselling and this makes it extremely difficult to know where to start. How could there be so many permutations and practices within one professional discipline! It does seem absurd; after all, there would never be that many ways to treat a physical illness. Such disparity and so little shared common ground among the approaches to psychotherapy mean that people in the field are themselves confused about what really works. For instance, those who offer cognitive-behavioural therapy (known as CBT) concentrate on the idea that changing unhelpful or realistic ways of thinking will help people change the behaviours that are stopping them from leading fulfilled lives. In person-centred therapy (the type most commonly on offer from counsellors in GP surgeries) the belief is that the solution lies hidden somewhere inside the suffering individual; so all the therapist has to do (the theory goes) is respectfully keep listening to the person talk, with a few prods in particular directions here and there, and they'll sort it all out for themselves.

> 66 We cannot be excessively angry ... if our needs are being fully met and we're using our innate resources properly. 99

By contrast, psychodynamic therapies operate from the belief that you have to dig up all past pains and insecurities and major disappointments to understand and overcome mental ill health. Each of these take a piecemeal approach and, consequently, some, albeit unwittingly, may do more harm than good.

Many of these different schools of therapy have got hold of a part of the truth but, unfortunately, they stick to that one part and hone it, to the exclusion of everything else. This tends to unbalance the work of therapists, however well meaning, who work from within such limited models. Of course, it is good to set people tasks to help them change problem behaviours or to help people become aware of and question negative thinking or to listen to people with empathy, *but none of these approaches is sufficient on its own.*

The human givens approach to psychotherapy and counselling (which we teach at MindFields College*) is *not* piecemeal. It is an holistic, bio-psycho-social approach, with one strong, overarching idea at its core: we cannot be excessively angry, anxious, depressed or in the grip of any other form of mental ill health if our needs are being fully met and we are making proper use of our innate resources. Human givens therapists don't diagnose deficiencies in a *person* but rather the deficiencies in their lives or circumstances that are preventing them from getting their essential needs met and/or using their innate guidance system effectively to meet those needs.

---

* To find a human givens therapist close to your area, call MindFields College on +44 (0)1323 811440 or visit www.hgi.org.uk/register/

Having established what is required, we then use a variety of tried and tested techniques to help people achieve that end, as quickly as possible. Unlike so many other schools of psychotherapy, we don't have one 'model' that we stick to like limpets and which we force everyone to fit. We work with what we see and learn from the individual in front of us.

How to find an effective counsellor

People are often confused by the difference between the terms psychotherapist and counsellor, as you will come across both. But, essentially, there is no difference between them, which is why we use the terms interchangeably. How practitioners style themselves is usually just a matter of personal preference (for instance, some think the term counsellor sounds more friendly; others think the term psychotherapist sounds more professional).

Newspaper and magazine articles on the subject of seeking therapy usually recommend that you check the register of certain organisations that accredit or register psychotherapists and counsellors. But, although well intentioned, this is not necessarily the best advice. How much training people have had, or which professional bodies they belong to, gives you no guarantee of their effectiveness as a therapist. Indeed, if practitioners stick rigidly to one model of therapy, as described above, they are not at all likely to be as effective as they could be.

The main point to remember is that whether people call themselves psychotherapists or counsellors, they will all encounter the same range of human distress in their work. All that really matters is how effective they are at helping other people.

Effective counselling checklist

We stress that an effective psychotherapist or counsellor will:

- understand depression and how to lift people out of it
- help immediately with anger and anxiety problems, including trauma (post traumatic stress disorder) or other fear-related symptoms
- be prepared to give advice if needed or asked for
- not use jargon or 'psychobabble'
- not dwell unduly on the past
- be supportive when difficult feelings emerge, but not encourage people to remain in an emotionally aroused state
- assist individuals in developing social skills (when appropriate), so that their needs for affection, friendship, pleasure, intimacy, connection to the wider community, etc can be better fulfilled
- help people to draw on their own resources (which may prove greater than they thought)

- be considerate of the effects of counselling on the people close to the individual concerned

- induce and teach deep relaxation

- help people think about their problems in a new and more empowering way

- use a wide range of techniques

- may set tasks to be done between sessions

- take as few sessions as possible

- increase self-confidence and independence and make sure clients feel better after every consultation.

Therapists who work in tune with the human givens (whether or not they are human givens therapists) always work in these ways. There are some other important aspects to consider, too, when making your choice.

Spare capacity

Whatever type of therapist you see, you need to be sure that they have the 'spare capacity' to work with you. Those who are preoccupied with their own personal concerns or troubles will not be able to distance themselves sufficiently to work with yours. You will have to use your own judgement and instinct in deciding whether this is the case or not, but there is much to be gleaned from someone's manner – are they relaxed, warm and comfortable to be with, for instance, or slightly anxious or brittle? Do they give you their full attention or are they too full of themselves and seeking attention from *you*? Are they, perhaps, too keen to push you to talk about (or not talk about) certain issues, which may reflect their own unresolved concerns? Remember, the therapist's responsibility is to work to help you. You should not feel that you need to accommodate the therapist.

Your reality, not theirs

Some people think that they need to see a therapist who comes from the same background or has the same sort of life experience, or has even experienced the same kind of trauma or discrimination as they themselves have – otherwise how will the therapist understand where they are 'coming from'?

But this is quite irrelevant in the human givens approach. Because the emphasis is on what clients can do to meet their *own* needs, human givens therapists can work with anyone. What you wish to

> 66 The therapist's responsibility is to work to help *you*. 99

achieve or change in your life is *your* decision. It doesn't make any difference whether you are younger or older, from a different ethnic background, have a different religion or a different sexual orientation from the therapist you see. You establish, with their help, which needs are not being met in *your* life and set *your* own goals. The reality or world they are concerned with is yours, not theirs.

Working the way the brain works

High on the list of our important 'givens' is the ability to relax and imagine and think creatively. Human givens therapists 'tap into' their clients' innate ability to relax deeply and make use of that relaxed state both to introduce positive suggestions and ideas and to help people use their imaginations to rehearse success in new skills. When you are relaxed, the right (visual, more intuitive) hemisphere of your brain is dominant, while the left hemisphere (which is more involved in language, analysis and rational thought) takes a break. It is the right hemisphere that is active when we dream, and its natural way of working is through metaphor. (We are using metaphor whenever we say something tastes or looks or sounds like something else.) Metaphors conjure up pictures and sensations that the more imaginative right hemisphere can instantly relate to. And, by bypassing the often resistant or negative rational part of our brains, we can take on board new ideas and useful analogies.

This is why metaphor is used a great deal in the human givens approach. To a young woman who loves nature and who has struggled throughout her life because of childhood abuse, talk of 'rooting' new ideas or 'fertile soil in which a fragile flower can at last flourish and grow strong' can be powerful indeed. Similarly, someone who is held back in their work life through fear of taking risks, and who happens to be a keen swimmer, may respond to the idea of 'taking the plunge' and an image of rivers flowing freely. Stories are the kings and queens of metaphor, and much can be achieved instantly with an apposite tale that might otherwise have taken weeks. Tales of overcoming misfortune, heroic acts, kindness that triumphs, loyalty that never wavers, dreams that, with hard work and belief, come true – these connect with us through our natural pattern-matching facility and lead us unconsciously to make the link between the metaphor or story and our life.

The rewind technique – a speedy treatment for psychological trauma and phobias

All human givens therapists are taught how to use the rewind technique,* a safe and swift method of neutralising high emotional arousal which has prevented the memory of a traumatic event from being processed as something that is in the past. Thus the trauma continues to impinge on every-day life in the form of intrusive memories, nightmares and constant unidentified anxiety. Sufferers are often much more prone to unstable moods and outbursts of anger.

---

* The original version of this technique was developed in America by the founders of Neuro-Linguistic Programming (NLP), after studying the hypnotic techniques of Milton H Erickson. By discovering *why* it worked, we were able to adapt and refine the technique to ensure more consistent results.

We, and other human givens therapists, have used the technique with great success, and often in one session, to resolve PTSD caused by traumatic events such as being caught up in car accidents, rail disasters, bomb attacks, near drownings, fires, horrific industrial accidents, vicious personal attacks, bungled operations, severe sexual and physical abuse, and so on. It is also a successful means of eliminating the high anxiety associated with phobias and the compulsion to carry out rituals. The rewind technique should be performed by an experienced practitioner, and only when you are in a state of deep relaxation. (See box opposite).

Although there are other ways of working with trauma, we personally favour the rewind technique, because, through lengthy experience, we know that a skilled therapist can use the technique to detraumatise a whole range of traumas in just one rewind, without these needing to be verbalised in turn or even necessarily brought to consciousness. Another advantage of the rewind technique is that a profound level of calmness is induced in the patient *beforehand*, with the effect that their emotional arousal can more easily be kept down once the patient gets in touch with the traumatic event. We also monitor our patients' emotional state closely throughout and, if their arousal increases and they get upset, we can gently guide them to take a break from 'viewing' the traumatic event and return in their imagination to the 'safe place'

The stages of the rewind technique

THE REWIND technique is performed when you are in a state of deep relaxation. Once you are calm and deeply relaxed, you are asked to recall or imagine a place where you feel totally safe and, with the aid of the therapist's promptings, to 'see' (for instance, the shady wood, the white sandy beach, the pale blue sea, the snow-covered mountains), 'hear' (for instance, the breaking of waves, the rustle of leaves, birds singing) 'smell' (for instance, the salty air, the perfume of flowers) and 'experience the textures' (for instance, the feel of the sand between your toes, the touch of a leaf) that you associate with that place.

You are asked to imagine that a TV set and a video or DVD player with a remote control facility appears in the beautiful surroundings you have conjured up in your imagination. Next, you are asked to 'float' to one side of yourself, out of your body, and to watch yourself watching the screen, without actually seeing the picture. (The therapist calls this a 'double disassociation'; it is a means of creating significant emotional distance from the traumatic memories so that they can be approached relatively calmly.)

You are then asked to watch yourself watching a 'film' of the traumatic event speeded up in fast-forward mode. The film begins at a point before the event occurred, when you didn't know anything terrible was going to happen, and ends at a point at which the event is over and you feel safe again.

Next, you are asked, in your imagination, to float back into your body and experience yourself going swiftly backwards through the traumatic event, from safe point to safe point, as if you were ▶

identified prior to starting the procedure. In this way we have a means of preventing a person from becoming too fearful and emotional, which is absolutely crucial for the success of the technique. It is also easy to integrate other therapeutic procedures with the rewind technique, while the person is still in a deeply relaxed state, such as the use of empowering metaphors and storytelling and the rehearsing of new learning.

However, it is important to be aware that, although the rewind has an extremely high success rate, we occasionally

a character in a video that is being rewound. Then you watch the same images but as if you are looking at the TV screen while pressing the fast forward button. All this is repeated back and forth, as quickly as possible, and as many times as needed, till the scenes evoke no emotion in you.

Afterwards, if the feared circumstance is one that will be confronted again in the future – for instance, driving a car, using the underground or seeing someone who once abused you – you are asked, while still relaxed, to imagine a scenario in which you are feeling relaxed and confident while doing so.

Besides being safe, quick and painless, this technique has the advantage of being non-voyeuristic. Any intimate details that you don't want to talk about – or any details at all – can remain private, because they are your memories and it is only *you* who watches the 'film'. ●

A full explanation of why this technique works so well can be found in our book *Human Givens: A new approach to emotional health and clear thinking.*

come across people for whom it doesn't work so well or doesn't work at all – particularly those who have difficulty relaxing deeply or getting in touch with feelings associated with the original trauma. People on the autistic spectrum, for example, whose brains don't seem to store, or have access to, specific emotional memories in the usual way, may not respond well to this treatment.

Therapy that works

As we have seen, the human givens approach takes into account the full range of human nature and needs. So, to give you a flavour of how therapy from this approach works, on the following pages we describe the ways that several human givens therapists have helped people help themselves with a range of anger problems.

Struggling for a work–life balance

Gloria was petite and had a gentle manner. So it was quite a surprise to Julian to learn, when she came to see him, that, the previous week, she had hit a shoe-shop assistant over the head with a boot, because she had felt she was being ignored. She told Julian she had heard a voice in her head, screaming, "Teach the bitch a lesson!" Although Gloria had never done such an aggressive thing before, it soon emerged that she was having increasing difficulty controlling her anger. It had first started to cause problems a year before, when she went back to work after having her fourth child, a second son. She already had two teenage daughters and a 10-year-old son from a previous marriage.

Gloria's husband had been made redundant from his job and, as she was the higher earner (she had a well-paid managerial job in the telecoms industry), they had agreed that he would look after the baby while she became the sole breadwinner. Her job was demanding and, most evenings, she didn't arrive home till gone 8 pm. She described how, soon after arriving home, she would frequently 'lose it' over something trivial, such as finding the washing up not done or that her daughters had left their clothes lying around, or that her older son's football boots were left caked with mud. And after longing all day to see her baby son, she would find that she was too exhausted to cope with him, if he was still awake, but was resentful if he was asleep. She would pick arguments with her husband and complain that he wasn't doing his domestic duties well enough. This shocked her because she had never been overly house proud before.

There were several consequences of all this. A serious rift was developing between her and her husband; her baby son seemed wary of her and didn't run to her for cuddles, as he had used to; and her daughters seemed to be spending lengthening periods of time in their bedrooms, away from the family. Gloria missed the former closeness she had enjoyed with them but also resented the fact that they didn't do more to help with their baby brother. She knew she was being unreasonable in all her demands and resentments and felt that, if she continued in the way she was going for much longer, her marriage and her relationship with her children would be in serious jeopardy. (Her relationship with her older son, she was relieved to say, at present seemed unaffected, but only because so much of his energy was directed towards his football.)

> 66 She knew she was being unreasonable in all her demands and resentments ... 99

Julian knew that the emotional withdrawal of Gloria's daughters was typical adolescent behaviour, so he tackled that concern first. He discussed with Gloria healthy emotional development, the changing role of a parent through a child's adolescence and the importance of continuing to be emotionally available to her daughters, in new but less overt ways. In doing this, he 'normalised' Gloria's experience, stopping her from feeling guilty and responsible for the change.

Julian then explained how a build-up of stress can lead to anger outbursts and how, once aroused, anger can badly affect our judgement and clear thinking.

He proceeded to teach her effective anger management techniques. "Do you recognise when you are becoming angry?"

he asked. Gloria said that she did. "Then, the minute you become aware that you are getting annoyed, distract yourself from what you are feeling. Get the rational part of your brain doing something that, for the moment, requires your full attention. For instance, mentally list 10 different colours, or 20 countries or five fruits beginning with a particular letter. Spend just 10 to 12 seconds doing that, and you can stop the emotional brain exploding with anger and hijacking your thinking brain! Then you can make a proper decision about whether you really want to mention the washing up or the clothes, or not."

Julian also stressed how important it was for Gloria to learn how to calm herself down whenever she needed to, and that she could best do that by learning a relaxation technique. So Gloria agreed to a relaxation exercise, in which Julian taught her 7/11 breathing, and took her on some guided imagery, during which he also reinforced the main points from the session. While Gloria was still

66 Get the rational part of your brain doing something that requires your full attention ... 99

deeply relaxed, Julian invited her to visualise herself at home successfully putting the anger management techniques into action and staying calm during the times she normally found most stressful.

Julian and Gloria also discussed the possibility of creating, with her husband's agreement, 15 minutes of 'down time' when she came in from work each evening – the time that presented the biggest challenge. This would allow her to calm down fully from the day's stresses by practising, undisturbed, her 7/11 breathing.

> 66 She had quickly won back her baby's affection and her relationship with her husband was much improved. 99

Their second session took place a month later. Gloria was pleased to report back that she had been successful in using the anger management techniques she had learned, briefly taking time out to calm down, as suggested, and then returning to participate in family situations. She had quickly won back her baby son's affection and talked joyfully of him approaching her for a cuddle once again. Her relationship with her husband had much improved, as she had stopped criticising him, and she was more accepting of her daughters' behaviour.

At this second session, Gloria also mentioned how sad she felt that she was missing out on her second son's babyhood. Getting control of her anger had brought this into sharp focus for the first time. She was now able to see that, for her, it was more important to be the parent caring at home, even if she had the higher earning capability.

The third and final session took place five weeks later. Gloria told Julian that she had discussed her feelings with her husband and they had agreed that they were willing to manage on less money, enabling him to seek another job, while Gloria remained at home for the next few years. A couple of months later Gloria telephoned to let Julian know the good news that her husband had settled into a new job and they were all enjoying a much more settled family life, free from anger.

The angry rapper

Will, an extremely aggressive 15-year-old who was always losing his temper and getting into fights, was brought to see Pamela because of her long experience and success in working with challenging adolescents. Will, who had an ASBO, was confined in a secure unit and deemed such a danger to others that, when he was brought in for 'anger management', Pamela was told that, for her protection, a minder had to be outside her therapy room. After working hard to build rapport with Will over a couple of sessions (during which she discovered the only interest and obvious gift he had was as a rapper), she decided to see if she could get to the root of his uncontrollable anger. As, apparently, his anger would just erupt without any obvious rhyme or reason, she suspected it might be part of a molar memory.

To briefly recap the findings behind the molar memory conditioning theory (put forward by Joe, see page 69), when inappropriate anger keeps occurring and causing problems in someone's life, getting the person to experience and stay with that urge – but *not* act on it – can enable them to bring to mind a significant event from the past, most commonly from their childhood. If the problem is caused by a molar memory, the feeling they initially recall on remembering the event is not the feeling of anger they started out with. But, by staying focused on the anger, it will eventually manifest itself in connection with the memory as an emotion they had also experienced at that time, but had felt unable to express. Getting the person to express it in the way they would like to have done at the time puts it back in proper context, so that it ceases to come up at inappropriate times anymore.

In the theory, Joe suggests that some painful or traumatic memories have roots in both pleasure (which includes anger) and pain. The pleasure element is suppressed because of the overriding pain (for instance, the shame of being discovered by a parent while acting 'inappropriately' in some way). When a crude pattern match to this situation occurs in the future, the brain accesses the pain memory first, to gauge what risk there will be to us, if we indulge the display of anger. Only if the risk is not 'life-threatening' (for instance, this time there is no one there to see, thus no embarrassment or shame), will the pleasure be sought instinctively, and thus usually inappropriately.

Knowing all this, Pamela asked Will to get in touch with the feeling of anger (which was extremely easy for him to do) and then to close his eyes, stay with the feeling and see where it took him. After a few moments he recalled an occasion in his bedroom at home, when he was six or seven. His father had come in, drunk, beaten him up, snatched the precious book in which Will wrote all his lyrics and torn up all the pages, calling his songs "rubbish".

"What did you do?" Pamela asked Will. "Nothing. I was frightened of him. I felt completely helpless." By staying with the original feeling of anger, however, he realised that he had not just felt helpless. He had felt fury with his father too, although he had not expressed it. By this time, he was deeply caught up in his memory. Pamela encouraged him to say to his father now what he wished he had said then. With tears pouring down his face, Will said, "How *could* you have done that to me? I wanted you to be proud of me and what I was writing! I wanted you to say, 'What are you doing, son? Would you let me read it? Wow, that's really good! Why don't you sing it to me?' Instead, you just rubbished everything I'd done, everything I am!"

> " The effect of this work with Will was amazing ... "

Suddenly, Will's angry behaviour made sense to Pamela. Will had felt utterly helpless in the face of authority (his father) when he was younger and now automatically reacted with anger in his dealings with authority – of which there were very many. (In his unconscious 'risk assessment', he would have realised that he wasn't helpless anymore; he was a big lad and could fight back.) Thus there was continual escalation of the problem, as more and more punitive authority figures inevitably became involved in his life.

The effect of this work with Will was amazing. Once he had expressed what he would have wanted to say to his father, had he not been so shocked and

> 66 ... he stopped getting angry and violent altogether. 99

scared when his song book was torn up, the anger that had brewed up, in the face of his helplessness, and had boiled over ever since was able to be put back where it belonged – in the past, along with that unpleasant memory. He stopped getting angry and violent altogether.

At their next and last session, Pamela challenged him, "Well, now, Will, if you are so good at it, can you write a rap for me, here, now, on the spot?" So Will did. And, unlike his dad's reaction, Pamela's response was, "Wow! Have you really done it, already? Can I read it? Hey, that's *really* good! Can I hear you sing it for me?"

Will became so polite and respectful after that that he was quickly moved out of the secure unit into foster care, where he has successfully re-built his life as a wanted member of a family.

Rewards and punishments

When Alan, a warehouse manager whose anger was getting dangerously out of control, first came to Mark for help, there was little of his house that remained undamaged by his fists or feet. And his partner, to whom he was supposed to be getting married, was threatening to leave him. For some time, Alan had been denying that he had a problem. It was only at the continual urging of his fiancée that he finally agreed to seek help and, by the time he arrived to see Mark, he was very upset about his lack of control.

Mark asked when it was that Alan lost his temper. Alan replied at once, "All the time." "So, you lose your temper at work, with your boss?" "Ah, no, not with my boss." "With your colleagues?" "Er, no." Nor, Alan realised, did he lose his temper with family or friends, although he could get a bit edgy with them. When he thought about it more closely, with prompting from Mark, he recognised that his out-of-control anger only occurred at home and only with his fiancée , and it was always about the little annoyances of domestic life. Mark then helped Alan realise that he was already exerting a degree of control over his anger, in that he chose where he would unleash it – at home, where he felt safest and most accepted. But his fiancée was not accepting anymore.

So Mark asked Alan what he thought would happen if he carried on in the way he was going. Alan admitted that he feared it was only a matter of time before he became physi-cally violent towards his fiancée. He would lose the person he loved and would have nothing left of value in his life.

"If your anger *wasn't* there, would anything be missing from your life?" Mark asked, and then led Alan through how well his needs were being met. Nothing crucial was missing. He enjoyed his job, loved his fiancée and was looking forward to their life together and the plans they had made for the future. He was desperate to change his behaviour.

> **"** Alan feared it was only a matter of time before he became physically violent ... **"**

Mark taught Alan anger-manage-ment techniques of the type described in this book and, in relaxed guided imagery, had him rehearse controlling his anger when flashpoints occurred at home. However, Mark sensed that Alan still needed some further motivation to enable him to persist with making these changes to his behav-iour. Knowing that Alan had once been in the army and was therefore quite used to the idea of consequences for bad behaviour, Mark invited him to come up with a reward for himself, if he succeeded in controlling his anger till their next session in a fortnight – and a punishment, if he didn't. Initially Alan struggled to come up with either, so Mark asked him what he really looked forward to each week. "Watching TV on a Saturday night with my fiancée, while sharing a few beers and a curry," said Alan at once. So Mark suggested to him that his punishment could be to sacrifice this weekly pleasure, and his reward to keep it. Alan readily agreed.

As a further incentive, Mark proposed that his fiancée also be deprived of the much-enjoyed Saturday ritual, if he became angry. (He knew she would be willing to go along with that, as she had been the one who contacted Mark initially, desperate for help.) Alan was more reluctant to accept this, as it didn't seem fair on her, but Mark persisted in encouraging him to agree. The fact that David truly loved his partner and didn't want to deprive her of one of the now few pleasurable times they spent together would create a particularly powerful incentive to deal appropriately with his anger. And, as yet another incentive, now that he was in the swing of it, Alan agreed that an angry outburst would also lead to a ban on sex for two weeks, as sex was something else that was good about the relationship.

> 66 Alan had a big smile on his face. 99

By the end of the session Alan had a big smile on his face. He said, "This punishment idea really finds out who you are, doesn't it?"

For he realised that the effectiveness of the strategy lay not just in the unpleasantness of the chosen punishment, but in what the actual carrying out of the punishment represented. For him, with a house smashed to pieces and a partner about to walk out in fear of her life, the 'punishment' he had chosen symbolised a devastating real-life consequence.

Two weeks later, Alan reported back positively. He admitted that he had become angry once, but did not get aroused to the usual level. He took time out, going for a long walk to calm himself down and, while out, decided that, given this dramatic improvement, he had earned his reward. Mark saw him again a month later, and still there had been no need for the punishments to kick in. Life was so much happier and more harmonious at home that Alan felt less and less desire to get angry.

> ❝ Life was so much happier ... he felt less and less desire to get angry. ❞

During the sessions he had also come to realise that his inappropriate anger stemmed from childhood, when, at around the same time, his parents divorced and he himself was diagnosed with diabetes. An unvoiced reaction of "It's not fair!" and "Why me?" had manifested itself in anger towards those closest to him, even over minor things such as whose turn it was to do the washing up or whether he had done it properly. Gradually, this had become habitual. However, he found – through the rewards and punishments idea – that he could let it go.

Mary's misplaced anger

Mary turned up for her first session with Christine at Hartlepool Mind only because her mental health support worker brought her; she rarely left the house and had felt unable to make the journey on her own. She was armed with a large box of tissues, which she needed, and she looked very sad and very tired. Her body language was defensive and she shook from head to toe; her gaze was riveted to the floor.

Mary told Christine through her tears that she had a miserable life. She lived with her son aged 16 and daughter aged 19 and, in her own words, "hated them both!" Mary hated her daughter because she was the cause of the intermittent pain she had had in her back since the daughter's birth and she hated her son because he was growing into a man and he looked like his father. They caused her constant upset and she could hardly stand being in the same room as them; this had resulted in the children spending most of their time in their own rooms. "It's as if they know I just can't be bothered with them," she said bitterly.

Mary had difficulties with anger, admitting that she could fly off the handle for no reason. She shouted a lot and was verbally abusive to her children a great deal of the time "because they deserve it". She said she couldn't relax and didn't sleep at night because of the constant pain in her limbs.

Mary couldn't remember much of her childhood but had a

memory of being used like a football and getting kicked all over the place. (She wasn't sure if this was an actual memory or a metaphor for how she had felt at that time.) She had been subjected to regular abuse by her grandfather from the age of 10 and felt that her mother could have stopped it but chose not to help, burying her head in the sand and denying anything was going on.

Her first husband (the father of her children) was extremely abusive and controlling; after a number of years she managed to end the relationship and met a new partner, who moved into the family home. He too became violent. This partner criticised her appearance and kept her a prisoner in her own home.

Once again Mary took control by ending the relationship and decided that she would have to manage on her own to bring the children up. She had clearly done a reasonable job. Her son was in sixth form college, hoping to go on to study for a degree and was highly creative and artistic. Her daughter was excelling in a very good career.

> **She said she hated both her children.**

When Christine asked Mary about the "hatred" she had for her children, Mary reiterated that she had no love for either of them because of all the pain and suffering they had put her through. They never gave a thought to her and how she was feeling. So, in return, she had tried to behave as if they weren't there.

Christine challenged this by asking if she had ever contacted social services to say she couldn't cope. Had her son been lonely with no friends, as presumably she wouldn't let him have anyone to the house? Was her daughter struggling at work because of all the tension at home? How had they coped without food being provided for them? How had they felt about having to wear unwashed clothing?

> **66 Christine then explained about trauma and pattern matching ... 99**

Mary looked horrified and said, "Oh no! I would never have phoned social services! Of course they had food on the table, clothes on their back and a warm bedroom to take their friends to when they visited!" She suddenly stopped looking at the floor and looked up. "I don't hate them, do I? I love them! But why do I feel such anger towards them both? They're actually the ones that are always there for me. I want them to care *about* me, not care *for* me!"

Christine then explained about trauma and pattern matching and the importance of relaxation and re-focusing negative thoughts. Mary stopped crying and started to listen. Christine gave her some coping skills to practise, such as recognising her flash points, using humour to break the anger trance and doing 7–11 breathing to bring down her anxiety levels. (Mary had refused to try a relaxation session there and then with

Christine, so Christine simply demonstrated what she should do in the privacy of her own home.)

The following week Mary attended the session without her support worker and was proud to say that she had travelled by bus and had practised her breathing to make sure she stayed calm. She looked happy and not one tear was shed throughout the session. Mary explained that she had realised that the anger she was feeling was aimed at the wrong people; her children did not deserve the continual verbal abuse they had been receiving from her. Mary had also started observing her children when they were around her and could see that they were both being very careful not to upset her. It was awful to her to realise that her children were scared of her, as she knew she would never intentionally hurt them. She had started spending time with them, talking to them and laughing when with them. Her daughter had remarked that she seemed much happier and that it was nice to see her being happy.

> 66 ... and how and why stress can cause hallucinations. 99

Mary had tried the relaxation techniques she had been shown and found them very helpful. She then disclosed that she had been seeing images of her abusers, which she had found distressing. Christine explained how and why stress can cause hallucinations, and Mary seemed relieved to hear that this could happen to anyone suffering with severe anxiety. Christine then reinforced the relaxation skills and explained how lowering stress in this way could help eliminate the images.

At the third session Mary turned up looking extremely well; with make-up and her hair tied back she looked 10 years younger than she had at their first meeting. Mary was happy and had lots to say about her week. It was obvious from her lively chat that she was engaging with life again

> 66 Mary looked extremely well and was engaging with life again ... 99

and was taking pleasure from socialising with a friend and going shopping with her daughter. She had also attended a musical at her son's college and had been so proud of him when he appeared on the stage. "I seemed to notice for the first time just how handsome he has become. I don't think I noticed it before – I was too busy looking for signs of his father in him!" she said.

Mary said she felt ready to try some guided imagery now, as she was still getting intrusive thoughts about her granddad. Christine explained the rewind technique and she agreed to give it a try. She seemed to respond very well to the technique and to the guided imagery afterwards in which Christine reinforced a positive expectation of her future relationship with her family.

Since then, Mary has continued making progress. She no

longer shouts all the time and, if she feels anger, she controls it by slowly breathing and refocusing until she calms down. She hasn't had any further episodes of seeing her abusers and believes that the associated emotions have been dealt with: in her own words, "I have found a filing cabinet for all the bad things that have happened to me. I have popped them in the drawer marked 'Do Not Disturb!' My hatred of those men has also been put in alongside them, where it belongs!"

Mary is now considering going to work or attending college herself. She is aware that she will sometimes feel stressed or anxious but is confident that she has the skills to deal with these emotions in the future.

Odd socks and heroes: bringing down emotional arousal

Seven-year-old Paul attends Fellside School in Cumbria for children who have faced complex challenging experiences in their past and have previously been deemed beyond help. Fellside is part of a residential therapeutic community, where staff work from the human givens approach.

Paul is a highly intelligent boy, with a reading age and comprehension level far in excess of his years but his behaviour can be impulsive. As David, his talented young key worker, describes it, "Suddenly, violent or aggressive outbursts will rock this little boy around an entire room, kicking and ripping all that falls into his path.

"When we first met Paul, he would lick people on the face, especially men. The face licking was as an attempt to put people in situations where they felt supremely uncomfortable and thus unsure how to react. He used this method to challenge authority and gain dominance – an extremely rudimentary but effective way of taking control of situations he found himself in. His upbringing would probably be described as difficult, but in all honesty should be described as unfair. He was neglected and rejected from an extremely young age by parents who lacked the ability to enable this young boy to flourish in any way, shape or form."

Paul is starting to flourish at Fellside and has supervised contact with his father. However, his mother (who is with a new partner) is now trying to re-establish contact with him, and this is causing him a great deal of inner emotional turmoil, along with broken sleep and vivid, unpleasant dreams. He knows he will never go back to either parent.

> " After his mother's visit Paul was violent and aggressive ... "

After his mother's first visit, Paul was violent and aggressive for a few days. People who worked with him described him as "on edge" and "wild", a far cry from the little boy whom they had found to be so full of intelligence and enthusiasm. In this outpouring of emotion, he smashed windows and toys, tore work and books, and kicked and scratched at people for the slightest of reasons.

Paul's mother's next visit was booked for just before Christmas, when she would be coming with her new partner and baby son, to give him presents. Staff ensured that Paul had time to walk into town and buy his mother a present. He was excited about giving her the toiletries set that he had picked out and bought for her with his own pocket money.

> 66 A far cry from the intelligent and enthusiastic little boy they knew. 99

In the days leading up to the visit, Paul's behaviour became slightly erratic, but he was able to be calmed down. On the morning of the visit, when David came to wake Paul, he found him looking tired. "I couldn't go to sleep because, every time I tried, the Woo Woos would come and start climbing up my wall," Paul said. 'Woo Woos' were his name for the shadows on the wall that he feared would jump out and get him. Usually his favourite teddy was powerful enough to save him from the Woo Woos, but on this occasion they had proved stronger than usual. David normalised this for Paul. "Sometimes, when we're feeling a bit anxious, ordinary things can seem bigger or scarier than they actually are."

It was quite accepted by Paul that David could have conversations with Teddy, so David was able to assure Paul that Teddy said he was still strong but would spend the day "pumping iron" to redouble his strength so that Paul could get on with his day and look forward to a brilliant night's sleep that night.

Paul was pleased, and his morning in class went well. He had threatened to break someone's pencil after he didn't get the seat that he really wanted, but had immediately apologised and chosen a different seat. (He was given the seat he first wanted in the following lesson, as recognition of his ability to control his emotional arousal.) But, as the time of his mother's visit drew near, he became increasingly agitated. Unable to concentrate on his schoolwork, he was taken up to his room to ensure it was tidy enough for his mother to give the thumbs up to when she arrived.

The visit itself went exceptionally well. Paul was thrilled with the remote-control car he received as a Christmas present, and his eyes lit up with pure joy when his mother exclaimed that the soap he had bought her was one of her favourites. He even got to play a few games with his baby brother, listening to his mother's instructions and at all times being careful and gentle.

When it was time for Paul's mum to go, she gave him a big hug at the door. "Stay for a bit longer!" he pleaded, but she was busy later on that afternoon and the drive home would take more than two hours. She had no idea when she could next come and visit, except that it wouldn't be until next year.

"I'll probably see you again soon," she said, as she took her leave. When she walked out, there were a few seconds of quiet. Then Paul cried, "Just one more hug!" and bolted towards the door. He didn't attempt to open the door by the handle, or even look through the window; instead, he began kicking the door as hard as he could, his whole body tense and clenched. Any attempts to talk to him fell on deaf ears, and he continued kicking out and shouting as he went up to his bedroom.

At that point, David was called. When he reached the door, he could hear nothing but crashing from the inside. His knock went unanswered, so he opened the door and went inside. There stood Paul on his bed, holding up his light-and-sound workbench above his head, ready to launch it toward the window. He spun around and looked, wide-eyed and unblinking, as David shouted his name.

> " ... he was about to launch the workbench through the window. "

"I have a huge problem!" David shouted, and fell suddenly to the floor, manically tugging at his shoelaces. When he looked up at Paul again, Paul was staring, his face already a bit softer. "I'll show you if I can just undo this," said David, quieter this time. "This is so embarrassing, and you're the only person in the world that I can show. My mother would kill me." He was speaking even more quietly now.

By this point Paul's curiosity had kicked in and the light-and-sound workbench was back down on the floor. "If you'll just jump down, I'll show you," David said. Within five seconds, Paul was standing next to him, fists clenched at his sides, towering over David as David writhed on the floor.

"You see," David explained, "Jumping on the bed looks like lots of fun, and so I want to come and have a go with you, but... [he pulled his left shoe off] this sock is green at the bottom and... [he pulled his right shoe off] this sock is yellow at the bottom. I can't get away with wearing odd socks! My Mum would kill me. What if I got run over by an ice-cream van on my way home and got taken to the hospital and they found ... odd socks!"

> 66 Something had to be done to lower his emotional arousal ... 99

Paul chuckled and sat down next to David. He pulled up his trousers, revealing one long black sock, and one slightly shorter, grey one. David whooped with delight. "We could be in the odd sock club!" he joked. "It's a shame that Teddy doesn't wear socks, or he could join our club too!"

Although they joked around a little, Paul was, of course, far from completely calm and relaxed. David was aware that, in order for Paul to be able go back to his normal routine for the rest of the day, something had to be done to lower his emotional arousal level. Catching sight of Paul's favourite computer game, featuring a young hero called Ben, David suggested that they go out for a walk and "play the computer game for real".

So off they went for a walk in the woods, David holding the imaginary pad of an imaginary computer game, shouting out which 'buttons' he was pressing, while Paul acted

> 66 On his return, Paul settled down and got on enthusiastically with his school work ... 99

out whatever the corresponding actions of the hero would be on the computer screen. David moved him through a whole range of imaginary situations that he conjured up, enabling Paul, as Ben, to jump and flip his way through the situations he encountered, defeating the 'monster of sadness' and the 'four-armed beast of confusion'. In this way, Paul could fight back against the things in his life that he couldn't control. The magic joy pad could even move the character of Ben backwards and forwards several times through the scenarios, enabling David to help Paul experience, in this innovative way, the emotional distancing achieved through the rewind technique (see page 197).

On return, Paul settled down into class and worked enthusiastically for the rest of the day. That evening he went to bed smiling and, in the morning, happily told everyone at breakfast how well he had slept the previous night.

David comments, "Since the last visit, our focus for Paul

has been on helping him come to terms with situations he cannot control. His mother's visits need to become periods of joy, rather than occasions that he has to drag himself back up from after she has left. From the start he has made, he appears to have a great chance."

The critical father

Twenty-five-year-old Lucille came to see Denise because, for the first time in her life, she was in a relationship with a man who meant the world to her, yet she kept having explosive and inexplicable outbursts of anger against him. "Ray is a lovely, gentle man; we get on really well and enjoy living together, and I *so* don't want to lose him," she said.

Lucille's parents had separated when she was eight. Her father was an extremely controlling man, with very firm views about right and wrong, and high expectations of his daughter's behaviour. He had been in the army and so was a stickler for discipline and for things being done correctly and thoroughly. He would bellow at, and sometimes hit, Lucille if she didn't lay the table neatly or sweep the floor properly or tidy her room well enough and, although she loved him, a lot of the time she was in deep fear of him.

She now worked as a legal executive but felt that wasn't 'good enough' and so was also studying to become a solicitor. Although she was aware that her outbursts were especially likely to happen when she was over-tired, she still felt that didn't totally explain them.

"I go off my head over tiny little things," she said. "I might come in and find that the cardigan I had left carefully over a chair back has been thrown casually on to another one, and sometimes that will make me just roar with temper. Or Ray will ask to borrow my car keys for 10 minutes because he can't find his, and I completely lose it. It drives me mad that he doesn't look after his own things and just expects to use mine!"

"Does he do that a lot?" Denise asked.

"Well, actually, no," said Lucille. "Hardly at all."

Denise agreed with Lucille's belief that stress was lowering her threshold for anger and asked if she enjoyed her studying. It emerged that Lucille enjoyed neither her job nor her studying but felt she had to 'prove' herself. And it quickly became clear that the person she felt she had to prove herself to was her hard-to-satisfy father, whom she saw once a month and who always seemed to think she could do better or try harder at everything she did.

> 66 I go off my head over tiny little things ... 99

Denise did a rewind on Lucille's traumatic childhood experience of abusive behaviour from her father. Then, while Lucille was still deeply relaxed, she asked her to bring to mind the last occasion when she had lost her temper with Ray over something minor and see if she could feel that same anger when she recalled it. Lucille nodded at once. She had no difficulty reactivating that anger. Wondering whether the outbursts might be related to a molar memory (see 'The angry rapper' on page 206), she asked Lucille to stay with the anger and see if any other memory came into her mind.

After a few minutes, Lucille nodded. She was remembering being sent to her bedroom at about six years old because she had done something which her father thought should have been done in a different way. She could no longer remember what that something was, but she remembered his rage and that he had hit her across the face. And she remembered sitting in her bedroom, feeling desperately lonely and confused. Denise asked her to stay with the feeling of anger that had brought this memory to mind, to see if anger was there, too, although she might not have expressed it or even been aware of it. A couple of moments later, Lucille nodded fiercely.

"Did you express that anger?"

"No, I didn't."

"If you could have expressed it then, what would the words have been?"

"I don't know."

"You were confused and hurt. Could you, perhaps, have been thinking, 'Dad, why are you behaving like this?' Could you try out some words and see if they feel right?"

"Dad, why are you behaving like this?" said Lucille softly

and uncertainly. And then, suddenly, her voice got stronger. "Dad, how *dare* you treat me like this! How *dare* you hurt me and make me scared of you! I'm only a little girl. Why can't I do things the way *I* want to do them, sometimes? Why is nothing I do ever good enough for you?"

Lucille's seemingly inexplicable anger outbursts against Ray now made sense. As an adult, no longer at risk of being yelled at or slapped (Ray would never behave that way), she had, unknowingly, at last felt safe enough to react angrily if things were not done the way *she* wanted – and that unconscious, irrational reaction, caused by the molar memory, had been creating all her difficulties.

> 66 She reminded Lucille of the many strong resources she had available to her ... 99

By this point, tears were pouring down Lucille's face. So Denise gently brought Lucille back to the 'special place' she had chosen for the rewind – an Italian beach on a hot day – and encouraged her to enjoy relaxing there while she reminded Lucille of the many strong resources she had available to her – her ability to be accepting, to form loving, supportive relationships, to apply herself, to want to do things to a high standard, to forgive, and so forth. Then, to show her that it was possible to put to use *in her own way* the values her father had wanted to instil in her, she told her the true story of Fisher, a man born in the early 1930s in what was then Rhodesia.*

The story begins before his birth. Fisher's parents, black Africans, had been forced, like all others, to give their land to the white colonisers and work it for them, for a tiny pittance (most of which they then had to pay back in tax along with a portion of the crops they had grown). One day, Fisher's father rebelled and ran away when the Bwana (white man) came to the village to collect his 'dues'. The Bwana was so enraged that he ordered Fisher's mother, at the time heavily pregnant with Fisher, to walk ahead of his horse, on a blisteringly hot day, to his own homestead 15 kilometres away, where he was planning to keep her until Fisher's father turned up with what he owed. He also threatened that, if he didn't turn up, she would never see her family again. Luckily for this terrified woman, a brave cousin rescued her and they returned, on foot, in the baking heat to her home. Not surprisingly, after all that exertion and stress, she gave birth almost immediately.

> 66 Lucille smiled and said she felt no anger at all ... 99

In the tribe from which Fisher came, it was the tradition that, when a child is born under unusual circumstances, its name must commemorate the event. So the baby was named

---

* This is a shortened version of the story told by Sheila Mudadi-Billings at one of the *Stories that Heal* workshop run for MindFields College by Pat Williams. A fuller version appears in "Patterns that persist: how childhood stories cast forward shadows" by Pat Williams (*Human Givens*, vol 14, no 1, 2007).

Fisher because that was the Bwana's name. The tribes people knew that attributes can be used for good or ill and trusted that Fisher could make good out of the qualities – tenacity, self-belief, single-mindedness, determination and conviction – which the Bwana himself had used so selfishly and unkindly, and that the young one would add to them his own humanity, kindness and generosity. And that is what young Fisher did. Despite being born into poverty and forced to leave school at the age of 10 to help his family, he undertook many challenges, overcame major obstacles and ended up building a thriving business that enabled him to give his own children the best chances in life. He transformed the Bwana's qualities into noble ones that enabled others to prosper.

Afterwards, Denise asked Lucille to think back to that last outburst with Ray and see if she still felt the same anger rising. Lucille smiled and said she felt no anger at all. A fortnight later, she emailed Denise to say that the anger she had felt so at the mercy of "had ceased to feel 'live' anymore". She was now also seriously rethinking whether she wished to become a lawyer and considering training to be a nurse instead.

"Don't come back"

Seven-year-old Faisal was brought to see Pat because of his towering rages. Faisal's parents had divorced when he was two, and the tantrums, which had begun then, had since escalated into frightening anger storms. When the rages erupted, he would trash the room, throw or smash whatever was near him, and hit out wildly at the people around him. Over the previous three years his mother had consulted many health professionals and also an anger management expert, but nothing seemed to help. She told Pat, "The anger expert said that, when Faisal felt a rage coming on, he should 'take time out'. But how can he? He never knows when it's going to happen!"

"How horrible for you", Pat said, looking at Faisal. "I expect you must hate it." Faisal nodded miserably. "I bet you don't really want to be like that, do you?" Pat continued. "It can't be much fun."

"No," Faisal said. "It isn't. It's awful."

"Well, that's okay then, because you know it's *not* you, don't you?"

Faisal looked up with interest and surprise. Rapport had been quickly established with Pat's first two questions, and now, with the third, Pat had his complete attention. "Well it can't be you, can it?" explained Pat. "I mean, this angry thing comes and goes, but you're there the whole time, so it can't be *you*, can it?" Faisal's expression, on hearing these words, was one of both curiosity and immense relief.

"So what does this angry thing which isn't you look like?" said Pat. "If he was a person, or a creature, standing way over there, what would he look like? What would you see?" Very slowly, Faisal came up with his answer: a huge looming shape of shifting blurry reds and blacks, and sharp and jagged edges. "Okay. Now give it a name. What do you want to call him?" said Pat.

Faisal couldn't think. "Any name you like," Pat prompted. "Mr Angry, Mr Red-And-Black-Blur ... even George, if you like."

Faisal brightened. "That's it. I'll call him George!"

"Right. Now that you know he has a name, maybe you'll be able to tell when he's coming." Pat described ways Faisal might notice that George was on his way – physical changes, such as starting to feel restless and sweaty, breathing fast, etc. "So, from now on, see if you can tell when George is on his way. And when you find you can do that, then phone and let me know," Pat said.

Three days later, Faisal's mum phoned. "He's started to say 'George is coming!' " she said excitedly, and put Faisal on the line. Pat said, "So you know when George is coming now! That's brilliant. The next thing is to see what trick you can find to stop him landing on you. I don't know what that will be, but I know how much you don't want George to land on you, and I'll bet you'll find some way of stopping him. When you find it, ring me up again."

> 66 This angry thing comes and goes, but you're there the whole time, so it can't be you, can it? 99

It took just another three days before Faisal was back on the phone. "You've found a way to stop George!" Pat cried. "That's wonderful! How do you do that?" Faisal joyfully replied, "Whenever I say that George is coming we all get together, whoever's in the house [it was a big family] and we chant!"

"Gosh. Do you chant anything you feel like, or something special?"

"We chant 'George, George, go away. *Don't* come back another day!' We chant it like that nursery rhyme – 'Rain, rain, go away. Come back another day!' But we go faster and faster and get louder and louder!"

Pat marvelled at the great solution Faisal had managed to come up with. To chant at George meant that Faisal had to be in his 'observing self', 'looking' at George from the outside, and that meant he couldn't be swallowed up in the rage. And the increasing speed and volume of the chanting soon led to laughing. George didn't stand a chance against all that ridicule.

After that, there was just one final step to take. Faisal was anxious about coping at school. "It's OK at home. But what if I feel George coming in the middle of a lesson? I can't start chanting!"

"Oh, you can still do it," said Pat, "but in a slightly differ-ent way. Remember when you learned to read; first you had to do it out loud, but later you could do it in your head. That was just as good, wasn't it? In some ways, it was even better. It's the same with chanting. When George comes, just chant inside your head. George will certainly hear you. You're absolutely brilliant to have thought of this idea in the first place. I think you'll do it just as brilliantly at school."

And Faisal did.

Fear that ended in violence

Cashel is 45, the youngest of a family of six children born and bred in a small town in Ireland. As a quiet and vulnerable child, he had felt helpless to escape either the violence inflicted on him within the family or the witnessing of that inflicted on others, notably his mother. His mother was loving but, as a victim herself, was unable to protect him, and he came to feel that, in the environment where he was growing up, the best form of defence was attack. This set his future pattern. His ambition was to become a gangster and make people fear him and in this he seems to have been highly successful. As a consequence, however, he had at times spent years in prison.

He first came to the attention of Paula when she was managing a project for people with drug and alcohol addiction. At the point where she started to work with Cashel he had been attending for some time, and was getting help with many of his needs, but he was still experiencing problems with relapsing into using heroin. He felt that he was using the drug as a way of preventing himself from falling back into extreme violence.

In their first session, she explained to him the cause and effects of trauma, as he simply felt that he was "just a head case". She told him how the high emotional arousal experienced during extremely traumatic events can prevent the experience from being coded properly in the brain as a normal memory. In effect, the event remains 'live' and any sound, smell, sight or experience that triggers unconscious recall of it will in turn trigger the fight-or-flight survival response. Cashel was extremely relieved at hearing this normalisation of his situation and even more relieved when Paula told him that there was a simple, effective treatment for it. He was able to see for the first time that the root of his violence was the extreme degree of fear he had experienced as a child.

> 66 Cashel was extremely relieved to hear this normalisation of his situation. 99

In their second session a week later they discussed Cashel's fear of his older brother, who had often been sadistically violent towards him. These experiences seemed to play a major part in his childhood trauma, colouring his memories of his home as a place to be feared and avoided. Although several family members seem to have been involved in the violence and the house would be smashed up in the process, experiences at the hands of this brother had a particular significance for Cashel, which Paula felt merited a rewind. This they did and Cashel can now recall his brother (who later committed suicide) with compassion, recognising that he also was a victim of his upbringing and circumstances.

> **He could now recall his brother with compassion ... he was also a victim of his upbringing and circumstances.**

In the third session they talked about Cashel's relationship with his mother and the fact that, despite her love for him, he remembered the family home as a cold, dark place, full of uncertainty and fear. He wanted to be free of these recollections and so, using guided visualisation, Paula asked him to revisit the house and, using whatever means he thought appropriate, to cleanse it room by room. She asked him to feel each room growing warmer and lighter as he cleared out all the old, negative feelings and, finally, to imagine taking his mother by the hand, standing with her outside the house and looking at it as a place filled with her love for him. He was very moved by this and subsequently remembered having actually lived there for a while with her in later life, having given her money with which she had redecorated the place. He described this as a happy time, which he had forgotten about but which had now become his dominant memory of home. He had also been able to go on to use this technique very successfully for himself, to change his feelings about other aspects of his childhood.

The next session focused mainly on the 'protective armour' he had built around himself and the way he experienced the world as a hostile place. In view of the positive changes he was making, he and Paula agreed that the armour no longer seemed useful. Again using visualisation, Paula suggested he see this protection literally as a suit of armour, weighing him down and separating him from experiencing his world directly, and to imagine removing it piece by piece. Afterwards, she asked him to provide himself with a form of protection that was light and flexible and allowed people and feelings in, and – knowing that this was a risky process for him – suggested that he would always know when it was safe and appropriate to let this happen.

> **" ... he was very pleased to have been able to react and behave differently. "**

In what turned out to be their final session they dealt with Cashel's concerns about his lifelong habit of acting on feelings with no thought for the consequences, specifically meeting any threat, whether real or imaginary, with extreme violence. He gave Paula a highly graphic description of one of the times when this had happened, with grave consequences, and expressed some amazement that no one had been killed. As he put it, at such times it was as if a wall came down and he couldn't see beyond it. Paula decided that the best way to approach this situation would be through a story.

Once he was deeply relaxed, she told him of a prince who lived in a castle with high walls. The prince was wilful, never listening to the voices of his advisers. He had a horse that he loved to ride in the surrounding countryside, which was green and luscious, with a river and cattle and sheep grazing. However, the prince liked riding only when the weather was warm and dry and so, on coming of age, he decreed that, henceforth, the weather would be permanently as he wanted it to be. After a time, his advisors became increasingly worried for him and for his kingdom but the prince continued to ride out, not noticing that it was harder and harder to encourage his horse to a gallop. One day he went to the stables as usual but did not find his horse saddled and waiting. His retainers fearfully told him that, although they had reserved as much hay and grain and water as they could to keep his horse going, it had finally succumbed to exhaustion and starvation like the rest of the animals. For, as there had been no rain, the crops had all failed and the river had dried up, leaving the kingdom devastated. The prince went up to the castle battlements, looked over and saw for the first time the devastated land and he wept for his folly and for the death of his horse. And, as he wept, the rain began to fall ... (Cashel had been tearful in his sessions, and was glad to find he could cry, as he had not been able to do so for a long time.)

Immediately after this session, Cashel was concerned that he had no memory of what had happened in it, but shortly afterwards, as Paula learned from his key worker, he had confirmation of its unconscious effect when he was confronted with a situation which would have had very unfortunate repercussions for him had he reacted to it in his former manner. He was very pleased that he had been able to foresee the consequences and, therefore, to react and behave differently.

" ... after 12 years in prison and 9 years of therapy, nothing has touched the core of my difficulties the way the human givens sessions have. "

Cashel still faces challenges but views life very differently and with a much changed perception of himself and his world. He has learned to value himself and acknowledge that he is a shy and sensitive man and that he can allow himself to be so, now that fear and brutality no longer determine his path. In an account of his experience which he wrote for Paula, he said, "During my life, I have been placed in assessment centres, institutions and prison. I have seen psychiatrists, psychologists, probation officers and social workers but the five human givens sessions I did centred my life beyond explanation, whereas the other interventions had only served to build up protective behaviour patterns which were very negative to my life and way of living. I was left feeling there was something profoundly wrong with me. I have been involved in violence all my life and it is only by the grace of God that no one has died. But there have been many victims of my

> 66 ... it has released me from years of suffering, as well as drug and alcohol abuse. 99

violence and I have to say that, after 12 years in prison and 9 years of therapy, nothing touched the core of my difficulties the way the human givens sessions did.

"I now recognise that I was suffering from post-traumatic stress disorder from an early age and that this form of therapy has at last released me from this and enabled me to achieve freedom from years of drug and alcohol abuse."

Change is easier than you think

We hope that, now you have reached the end of this book, you feel ready to tackle inappropriate anger with confidence. Doing so will transform your life and those of others close to you. Anger seems like a strong emotion but it is actually generated by fear – fear of loss, fear of being taken for granted, fear of being disrespected, fear of being hurt, fear of very many things. Out-of-control anger causes hurt and pain to all who are affected by it – perhaps, most particularly, you.

As we have shown, excessive anger, resulting in selfish or

aggressive behaviour, is an urgent signal that something is not working well for you in your life. You are not an angry person. You are only ever in the grip of anger. When you make the necessary moves to take back control over your life, ensure your needs are met in balance and make full use of your innate resources and learned skills (by using the guidance in this book and, perhaps, the help of an effective therapist), you will no longer have any need to feel or inflict the misery of inappropriate anger.

* * * * *

If you have found this book helpful, you might like to recommend it to friends or colleagues who could benefit from reading it too.

It's available through all good book shops or direct from HG Publishing on 01323 811662 or online at: www.humangivens.com

INDEX

How to lift depression... *fast*

How to lift depression... fast is published in paperback
by HG Publishing (2004) ISBN: 978-1-899398-41-6

Freedom from Addiction:
The secret behind successful
addiction busting

"Following *How to Lift Depression...fast* this second title is highly recommended. It sidesteps jargon, avoids the medicalisation of addictive behaviour, explodes the lies that maintain addiction and offers realistic, practical solutions."
Peter Barraclough, Nursing Standard

"So many books promise so much, and then fail to deliver. This book is of an entirely different quality. If you have an addiction/ compulsive behaviour, do yourself a big favour, buy it – it gives answers ... a big thank you to the authors." *Amazon Review*

"An easy-to-read, empowering self-help guide for those considering themselves 'addicted' to anything... It breaks down simply the self-assessment needed for discerning problem areas and their development, adding relevant research in a jargon-free manner; with a fascinating explanation for how neurophysiology and 'pattern-matching' underpin symptoms like craving."
Neia Glynn, The Psychologist

"Here is another excellent book from that groundbreaking team, Joe Griffin and Ivan Tyrrell. This time the focus is on addiction, how it comes about, and a highly effective way of dealing with it – whether it be a life threatening addiction (and many are) or an annoying habit which one would like to be rid of... There are techniques and ways of looking at problems which we can assimilate and pass on to our clients. *Freedom from Addiction* is easy to read, gives clear guidance and is an ideal book to have to hand to enable you to help yourself, your family, your friends and your clients." *Ruth Morozzo, 'Footnotes' Journal*

"Full of insights, this book is truly superb, not just in the area of understanding and managing addictions but also in providing a broader, clear, coherent and wholly convincing insight into human thought processes and behaviours." *Amazon Review*

Freedom from Addiction is published in paperback
by HG Publishing (2005) ISBN: 978-1-899398-46-1

How to Master Anxiety:
All you need to know to overcome stress, panic attacks, phobias, trauma, obsessions and more

"A wonderfully empowering book... full of practical advice."
Dr Gina Johnson, GP

"This book is a further wonderful aid. It throws, as it were, a rope to a drowning person. It gives the reader an immediate feeling that it is possible to take control again. And it is down-to-earth. The authors begin by explaining what is happening to us physiologically, emotionally and cognitively when we become anxious. They explain for example what is happening in our bodies when we are in an anxious state and over-breathing. The knowledge that the physical symptoms we experience are due to a greater or lesser degree of hyperventilation – and nothing more serious – itself has a calming effect. Similarly the knowledge that anxiety is a natural survival mechanism – the fight/flight response – helps our understanding of what is going on when we become aroused and anxious. Becoming aroused and anxious has in turn a profound effect on our thinking processes and our perspective on life. And the authors have masses of practical suggestions for bringing sanity to negative thinking processes.

Within the pages of this book you will find practical information about, and specific techniques for overcoming, generalised worry; poor sleep and how this can lead to depression; post-traumatic stress; obsessive compulsive disorder (OCD); panic attacks; agoraphobia; phobias; psychosis. There is also a variety of case studies — examples of people whose problems have been relieved.

Being given this book is like being given a key. It is based on scientific insights and is unemotional and immediately practical. It makes anxiety understandable and reversible"
Ruth Morozzo, 'Footnotes' Journal

"For anyone whose life is made miserable by excess anxiety, this book is worth its weight in gold. " *Amazon Review*

How to Master Anxiety is published in paperback
by HG Publishing (2007) ISBN: 978-1-899398-81-2

Dreaming Reality:
How dreaming keeps us sane
or can drive us mad

"*Dreaming Reality* exquisitely scythes through the Gordian knot created by past dream theories. Even better, like all the very best explanations, its central theme is as far-reaching as it is intuitive. Through a fascinating combination of dream examples and scientific findings, it provides lucid and compelling evidence for how our night and daydreams not only mould our personalities but also lie at the very heart of being human." *Dr Clive Bromhall, author of 'The Eternal Child'*

"A remarkable book that makes compelling reading. Griffin and Tyrrell's adroitly written text challenges traditional views on our knowledge and understanding of the mystifying covert world of dreams." *Professor Tony Charlton, Professor of Behavioural Studies, University of Gloucestershire*

"This book is revolutionary in more than one way. Past and sometimes overlooked research is re-evaluated, and a persuasive theory emerges... long overdue to my mind." *Doris Lessing*

"For anyone who has speculated on the meaning and purpose of dreaming, Griffin and Tyrrell's astounding insights light up the dark corners of the mind. Not since 1964 when Carl Jung's book *Man and his Symbols* was published has anyone set out to write so conclusively on dreaming for a wide audience.

Griffin and Tyrrell [propose] that dreaming functions to cleanse the undischarged emotional arousals of the day and they explain how this happens through metaphorical pattern-matching. From this one sets off on the journey to understanding the true causes of (and routes to healing) depression.

This book is revolutionary in thought, revelatory in content and will be established as the most important twenty-first century milestone on the road to accessible mental health treatment for all. It's a must for all who live with mental illness or work for its relief." *Ian Hunter* OBE

Dreaming Reality: How dreaming keeps us sane, or can drive us mad is published in paperback by HG Publishing (2006) ISBN: 978-1-899398-91-1

Human Givens:
A new approach to emotional health and clear thinking

"*Human Givens* is the most practical and intuitive book I've read in years." *Charles Hayes, Autodidactic Press, USA*

"Harnessed between these pages are scientific insights and practical techniques of sufficient power to completely revolutionise our approach to parenting, teaching and the caring professions. I wholeheartedly recommend *Human Givens* to any individual with a burning interest in how life works and can be helped to work better."
Dr Nick Baylis, University of Cambridge's Well-being Institute

"Griffin and Tyrrell's contribution advances psychology as much as the introduction of the Arabic numeric system with its zero digit advanced mathematics." *Washington Times*

"A quiet revolution." *New Scientist*   "Key insights." *Financial Times*

"Important original work ... both aesthetically pleasing and of immense practical use... has great relevance to all areas of life... could save (tax payers) millions of pounds. "
Dr Farouk Okhai, Consultant Psychiatrist in Psychotherapy

"A wonderfully fresh and stimulating view of dreaming, evolution, and human functioning. *Human Givens* also provides both an encompassing model and practical, specific applications to enhance the effectiveness of psychotherapy. It will deepen and widen every reader's perspective." *Arthur J. Deikman, M.D., Clinical Professor of Psychiatry, University of California*

"In *Human Givens* Griffin and Tyrrell offer innovative perspectives on promoting effective living. They have synthesized brain and social research in such a way that they provide new templates for understanding how to unlock the best in human nature."
Dr Jeffrey K. Zeig, Director of the Milton H. Erickson Foundation

"While books are never a cure for what ails us in life, they are often a catalyst, a trigger that fires off those rare and profound 'aha!' moments that lead to deeper insights and understanding. *Human Givens* is such a catalyst." *Jack Davies*

Human Givens is published in paperback
by HG Publishing (2004) ISBN: 978-1-899398-31-7